BRIGGO'S WORLD OF SPEEDWAY

SOUVENIR PRESS

First published 1973 by Souvenir Press Ltd., 95 Mortimer Street,
London, W.1, and simultaneously in Canada by J. M. Dent & Sons
(Canada) Ltd., Ontario, Canada

ISBN 0 285 62114 9

Filmset by Keyspools Ltd, Golborne, Lancashire
Printed in Great Britain by
C. Tinling and Co. Ltd., Prescot and London

Contents

Photographic contributions by Mike Patrick, Trevor Meeks, Alf Weedon, Cecil Bailey, Wright Wood, Dave Friedman, Mark Sennet, Helga Keilwerth, Mike Kilby, Franz Kellworth, Claude Salmon, Alan Seymour, the Daily Mirror and the Christchurch Star.

Welcome to my world...

ROAMING round the world, racing motorcycles, is sometimes tough, but usually a very enjoyable way of making a living. The sport has its black side, but the public sees only the glitter and glamour. With its increasing popularity on a world basis, speedway is emerging as one of the most exciting and keenly-followed of all sports. And the fans seem to enjoy every glimpse behind the scenes. More people complimented me on my autobiography *Briggo* which was published last year than on any world's championship I won. So here we go again — with pen to paper. It's another dimension of the racing world, but like most other aspects it is something I enjoy and I hope some of that comes across in this book. Speedway certainly doesn't stand still. There have been loads of changes even in the last twelve months; new techniques, different attitudes, fresh faces appearing on the scene. In *Briggo's World Of Speedway* we have chosen a selection of what we hope you will find to be interesting topics; and apart from my own opinions you will find contributions from my wife Junie, from my old friend and mentor Trevor Redmond, and Keith Goodwin, a London publicity agent who's been good to me and speedway. Once again Martin Rogers and Philip Rising have been vital cogs in the production team . . . and we hope you enjoy the fruits of our labours.

THAT BRIGGO!

by TREVOR REDMOND . . . see over

Trevor Redmond, the one-time guardian of Barry Briggs, with Briggo at Wimbledon.

I suppose it is fair to say that I know as much about Barry Briggs as he knows himself — probably more, as I have been associated with his career from the start. In fact, before the world came to hear of Briggs.

At 17 I had just sold my first motorcycle, a belt-drived Douglas, and replaced it with a 250cc model. Anxious to try it out, I decided on a run round the Cashmere Hill towards Halswell, near Christchurch, New Zealand. While out, I met another motorcyclist, George Gates, whom I had gone to school with, and his cousin. They were marking out a trials course on the roadside.

We all tried the course and I was impressed with this youngster. He could ride a bit. His name: Barry Briggs. This was our first introduction to competitive motorcycling, which

has taken us all round the world and into some adventurous and hair-raising experiences.

About a year later, I managed to acquire a half-mile dirt trotting track near Barry's home. We raced cars and motorcycles, but the local ACU stepped in and said as we were professionals, we must build a proper speedway stadium or close down.

We already had four motorcycle clubs in the town and didn't really need a fifth . . . but it was necessary to save *my* track, so I formed the Tai Tapu Motor Club. This club proved to be the upsurge of motorcycle racing in New Zealand and, I believe, world speedway.

Barry used to cycle to these meetings to help out. Excitement grew with the arrival of an Australian circus, with a Wall of Death. That excitement grew still further when a guy

An early New Zealand team in South Africa

named Les Moore leg-trailed his dirt Rudge at one of our meetings.

Ronnie, Les's son, and Barry became great friends — how's that for a bit of news? — and when Ron was 15 he had his first ride on a speedway machine at the Tai Tapu track. I used to do the announcing, tell a few jokes, and look after the cash. I'm good at that!

One week we decided to bring down some Midget cars from the North Island and that did it. I had these cars on show in town, which caused a terrific traffic jam and tipped off the Press about the great news event. After this, the speedway was built in Christchurch.

I invested all my money in a new machine and shares. Les Moore decided to stay in Christchurch and became a director of the speedway, while I joined him with the Wall of Death and on a great gold diving exhibition.

Barry and Ronnie were riding cycle-speedway together. Ronnie started to show up well at the new speedway while Barry helped in the pits. After some success against Norman and Jack Parker, the visiting English internationals, Les, Ron and myself decided, in 1950, to go to England.

After my first year in the U.K., where I had been successful with Aldershot in the third division, Barry cycled down to see me when I arrived back in New Zealand. I was proud to show him my new Austin A70 and Matchless twin motorcycles.

As Barry was keen to start riding, I gave him a pair of boots and a crash helmet. He later bought the boots to England but I still haven't found out what happened to that crash hat.

In 1952, Barry decided to come over to England to join me at Aldershot, but in the meantime I had been transferred to Wembley Lions for a record fee. He decided he would rather stay with us in Sutton and join Wimbledon, if possible. I managed to get a machine from Ronnie Greene and an assurance that he could go into the second division if he didn't make it. So he joined Wimbledon.

Barry was rather tall and awkward and it took some time trying high handlebars and low footrests, giving him advice to keep him in the team. Each week I had to have a diplomatic chat with Ronnie Greene, telling him Barry would soon go well, and that things like cracked pistons and bent frames weren't helping.

We started doing the tuning at home and I was head mechanic. There was no shed, and I can remember working under an old mac in the rain, swearing and trying to complete the machine with water running off us; and all about an hour before the meeting was due to start.

I wasn't the best rider, but I could always give good advice, and tell the boys what they were doing wrong.

On a visit to West Ham, Barry was very impressed with Jack Young (World Champion), who went round flat out without even putting his steel show down. Barry said that Youngie was great. I thought: I'll show them how good Youngie is, and tried to do the same.

I came into the bend flat out, keeping my weight well back, and my left leg up. In my opinion, I was doing a Youngie, until in the middle of a corner I hit a bump and practically landed on the dog track. After that I decided to continue as T.R. This really amused Barry when we discussed it in the dressing room later.

We also decided it was time for New Zealand to start racing as a team, so we pushed out a great deal of publicity, saying that at all these matches we would perform Maori hakas, etc.

Our first match was at Wimbledon and it was difficult to teach the riders the haka while they were warming up. You can imagine the chaotic scenes in the pits! After the introduction, all the riders came together for the famous Haka, and we had to make it up on the spot.

I used all the names of various mines and

mountains like Waikarimoana, Waimakarari and, each time I stopped, all the riders had to say *HOO* together. At the end we did a rhyme and leapt in the air. It went well and we were congratulated, people telling us we were better than the All Blacks.

We improved on it slightly and have entertained crowds all over the world with this speedway-style Haka.

We then took the New Zealanders to South Africa, where I started building stadiums. Barry gained great experience, and when he was made captain of a Test side he gained confidence, too.

We had some fun at the Kruger Park, when some Americans thought the Lions were attacking us. We had been taught by Fred Van Zyl how to do a lion's roar! In Durban we organised a Rickshaw race with the Zulus.

Barry won but was disqualified for helping to pull the cart. And, on our flight home, the plane broke down in the Sahara and we were stranded for five days.

Around that time, Sweden, could not break into international speedway and their riders had to come to England and race in the qualifying rounds of the World Championship. I organised the first international match in Sweden, and later in Poland, with the New Zealand and Australian riders.

We took along 'Waltzing Matilda' as our national anthem, and everyone saluted and stood to attention for this Aussie folk song . . . until the British Embassy heard about it. They sent a representative from Stockholm to Gothenburg to stop us.

At a party in Gothenburg, Olle Nygren and company put on a cabaret in the clothes of

Trevor Redmond, displaying his doubtful prowess as a 'matador' with Alan Quinn of Australia as the 'bull'. This contest took place in South Africa at a time when bullfighting was all the rage.

Ken McKinlay (left), Josef Hofmeister and Trevor Redmond at a World Team Cup meeting in West Germany.

the local promoter. Barry, Ron and myself did one of our (in)famous Hakas in our underpants. But the Aussies topped us all with Jack Young, Ray Cresp and Pete Moore coming on stage backwards as the three 'bums'.

Nobody would travel back to the hotel, some 80 miles away, with Ray Cresp, so I let Barry take my transporter and went with Ray. After 30 miles, we went round a corner too fast and crashed into a railway bridge at 70 mph. The Morris 1000 stood on end and the motorcycles fell on us, cutting open my face, breaking my heel and giving Ray concussion. I had about £1,000 in my pocket and thought . . . I can't die with this amount of cash about!

It was 3 a.m., and finally a car stopped and called an ambulance. Barry eventually found

us — in hospital. Ray stayed unconscious long enough to avoid taking the breathalyser. Barry and Ronnie took over the team, and the £1,000, and with my Ford Transit, six bikes and six riders, travelled from Sweden to Austria, 1,500 miles, in under 30 hours.

Professor Renisch was a great promoter in Austria. We raced at Linz, Graz and the 60,000 stadium in Vienna. On one trip he arranged a banquet with the Mayor Franz Jonas (now President of Austria) in the same famous rooms where Kruschev and Kennedy had their peace talks.

Ove Fundin was with Barry, Ronnie and myself on this occasion. We all agreed this was lifting speedway up to the Buckingham Palace level.

11

Phil Crump, winner of the 1972 Division Two Riders' Championship at Wimbledon. Phil, who rides for Kings Lynn, missed much of the 1973 season with a broken wrist.

Briggo writes about . . .

THE SPORT AND ME!

THE times are changing – in Speedway as in everything else. Techniques are altering, mostly for the better . . . mechanical refinements are improving all the time. The business is getting so competitive and so professional – at least as far as the attitude of the top riders is concerned – that everybody wants to be just one jump ahead of everybody else.

Elsewhere in the book I have examined lack of forward thinking and organisation which is shown in too many quarters; but to put the balance right, it has to be said that a lot of the boys are taking Speedway far more seriously than has been the case for many years.

Ole Olsen, who won the World Championship in 1971 and should have won it again last year but for a silly mistake, is leader of the seventies revolution. He is probably as fast a rider as there has ever been. Ole, the dashing Dane, has brought a new dimension to track tactics.

In some ways he plans his races like a motor racing driver. Graham Hill once said that the basic idea of driving a motor car fast was to go in straight lines wherever possible. Ole adopts a similar principle. Obviously the shorter the distance you travel, logically the quicker you arrive at that chequered flag. Mind you, the big handful merchants who screw on the throttle and do the spectacular round the boards manoeuvres are good to watch and very often you can get a better line going out wide – where the dirt is – than by sitting mid-track or holding the line.

But with the Olsen method the straighter you go, the quicker you go. And if that impetus can be maintained, it doesn't matter too much if the track is slick.

Promoters are pretty sparing with the old shale these days. I don't mind a slick circuit myself; most of us have become used to circuits like that anyway. But in big meetings especially, it becomes so important to get out of the gate first. Sometimes Ole is a terrific starter; other times not so hot. But he is probably better equipped than any rider in the World today to win races from the back.

He used to worry and panic if he didn't make the box and even now he is still prone to do some extraordinary things. But at least he has developed a technique and ability which enables him to go by even the most accomplished of opponents given half a chance.

It's a tight business, really. After all, most of us are riding virtually the same equipment. Although all the top boys have their own pet theories about what makes a bike go a fraction faster, in the end it's usually down to the bloke himself.

13

Ole, of course, goes down as a terrific disciple of Ivan Mauger, World title winner for three years before Olsen got his hands on it, and champion again last year.

Ivan was riding for Newcastle when Olsen came over as one of a party of several enthusiastic Danish youngsters in 1967. It was in a training school at Belle Vue, Manchester, that Ivan spotted Ole's potential. Many stories have been told about how Mauger recommended him to Newcastle because he could speak English better than any of the other boys; but if the truth be told, even then, Olsen's ability was noticeable.

Even more remarkable was his capacity to absorb information and to learn. For three years he was an almost constant companion of Ivan. They travelled to meetings together, worked on their bikes together, rode in the same team. Almost every mannerism that Ivan adopted, Ole would follow.

But he wasn't a slavish imitator. Certainly he borrowed the best of Ivan's theories, modelled himself to a large extent upon the man, worked hard at concentrating in the detached, ice cool fashion, that Mauger has made his trademark . . . but Ole had some ideas of his own, too.

The trouble was that for a long time he could never bring himself to believe in them. For months he lived in Ivan's shadow. Gradually, though, results started to improve. In the end it became clear to everybody that – carbon copy or no – Ole was going to be a very special rider.

Within a couple of years he was unmistakably world class himself. The fans up at Newcastle never left before the final race of the night – invariably it was a clash between Mauger and Olsen. At first Ivan won all the time. Then Ole started to win a few. But the middle of the 1969 season, the locals up there even reckoned that Olsen was definitely quicker than Ivan and certainly not too far behind him when it came to tactical awareness, either.

1970 was really the season that Ole grew up – and it came about after Ivan had asked for and been granted a close season transfer from Mike Parker's Newcastle track to Belle Vue. In many ways an important move for both men.

From Ole's point of view, the real significance of Mauger's going was that now he was the top boy. Quite possibly the place wasn't big enough to hold

the both of them anyway, not that that was the reason for Ivan wanting to get away.

He had his own problems with Promoter Parker but Ole, apparently, didn't have any such worries and one way and another he was more than happy to carry on at Brough Park.

He was established as the man upon all the others could, would and subsequently did lean, Olsen seemed to grow in stature both as a rider and a personality. The rough edges were coming off his fearless attacking style. What the Newcastle folk had been saying about him in the preceeding months became one of Speedways talking points.

Wherever you went, whether to Exeter or Manchester to Scotland or Swindon, it was Olsen the boys were discussing.

Newcastle fans had had a world champion to salute for two years running and for anybody wanting to put money on a good outside chance, it looked as though Olsen might make it three in a row for them. The odds were against him. While he was beating plenty of the top names with a fair amount of regularity in the League, his experience of big time meetings was still extremely limited. His temperament and ability to cope with those pressures was open to some question.

But nobody knew better than Ivan. The pressure was on him. Some of the boys had developed a bit of a thing about the difficulties of racing in Poland, and this was the first year in which the final was going to be held in that country.

Ole didn't have any such fears. It was new and exciting to him. He hadn't had time to get a fixation about places he didn't like; in fact for a comparative rookey in the big time stakes he was already as adaptable as almost anybody, whatever the conditions and circumstances.

The world final in Poland that year (Ole's first championship appearance) didn't altogether confirm that judgement. Magneto trouble spoiled the Dane's chances and he only mustered half a dozen points while Ivan went on to a brilliant fifteen point maximum which shattered all opposition.

The following season was a different story.

Two important developments took place during the Winter of 1970/71. First, Ole took himself and his new wife Ulla off to Australia to do the season out there. Then came the news that Newcastle wouldn't be operating again – and Mike Parker wanted Ole

Turning back the clock . . . Ivan Mauger (right) meets Bjorn Knutsson in 1966.

to go down to Wolverhampton, another of his tracks.

The Australian part of it was probably the most important. I would always encourage ambitious young riders to take a free-lancing trip down under if and when the opportunity presents itself. If the opportunity doesn't present itself, then manufacture such an opportunity. The Aussies always like riders who are good value, and they reckoned that they'd never seen anyone like Olsen. He was just terrific wherever he rode.

What is it about Aussie? Well, it is a tour which encourages, indeed demands, that a rider has to be self reliant. Ole clearly showed that he could handle himself. And some of the form he put together was further confirmation, if any were needed, that now he was in the Big League.

On his return came that switch into Wolverhampton. Whoever you are, and even if you're under the same or similar management as before, a switch of track is always a test. Ole has emerged as personality plus at Newcastle. Now he had to convince the Wolverhampton public, for about the departure of Swedish pin-up Hasse Holmkvist, that he was a man big enough to take over the mantle of Midlands top man.

It took Ole just about five minutes to do that. Bill Bridgett, who looks after Monmore Green, declared immediately that this fellow was the biggest and best thing ever to happen to Wilverhampton; it was a sentiment heartily and loudly endorsed by their fans.

Supporters elsewhere also saw an even more polished, competent and speedy Olsen. He snipped slices out of various track records up and down the country. Some of his form was really phenomenal. For him to be beaten at all was a rarity, so much so that that in itself became a talking point.

Now the pressure was really on Ivan once more. I had fouled up my own chances of being around for the World final by clanging ingloriously in the Nordic/British final up at Glasgow's Hampden Park.

So the field was clear for the two of them to fight it out in Gothenburg.

I really fancied Ivan to take the title. Even though Olsen was in such terrific form, there were still odd question marks about his big night temperament.

To win a World Championship, or at least to give yourself a fighting chance, you have to be capable of making five consistently good starts in the evening. I am not saying that gating is important above all, but Ivan had shown how essential the starts were.

He was the man who made them consistently. As it turned out, it didn't matter to Ole. In a couple of his races at Ullevi, he started like a novice. The other three were disappearing into the far distance by the time he got off the grid. Yet, using all his pace and power, he picked them off one by one.

Five starts, five wins, and Olsen was the World Champion for 1971 – at 24, the youngest man to win the crown for fourteen years . . . since I had got my first title, in fact, in 1957.

There is no doubt at all in my mind that Olsen is going to be around for a good while. It'll be no surprise if he wins as many titles as Ove Fundin, Ivan or myself have done. It will be more of a surprise if he doesn't.

Imitation, they say, is the sincerest form of flattery. And naturally enough, every rider nurses the dream that he too would like to be World Champion. Though not everybody is going to be able to adopt the Olsen style.

But there are boys around who will model themselves on him, who will adapt their techniques accordingly, and I can think of a couple of youngsters who have probably got what it takes to get up there and challenge for the big honours in the very near future.

Phil Crump, the 20 year old Australian from Kings Lynn, is one who springs to mind. Last year Phil was based in Cheshire, and spent a lot of time

at Ole's place at Holmes Chapel. You might say that he was a disciple of Olsen in much the way that Ole was of Ivan a few years ago.

But Crump, too, has a mind of his own. Nevertheless, he is prepared to use the best advice and guidance put his way. I decided to sponsor him this year because he is a good listener, a keen lad who is hungry for success and doesn't mind being told.

If I can help him it will probably be more in his attitude and mental approach than the actual style of riding. It is difficult to know where to start and finish with a rider's technique.

Crump is in the Olsen breed in that he too goes very quickly and very straight. It was good enough to make him far and away the leading rider in the second division last season, good enough to bring him bright results against quite a few of the first divisions most respected names. And despite trouble with a bad wrist injury, he kept fighting away and had the reward of the Second Division Riders championship at Wimbledon right at the end of the season.

It won't be the last important title the boy wins. I could see him going all the way to the top.

Gary Peterson, who rides at Wolverhampton and therefore has every chance to study Ole at close hand, is another good bet. Naturally enough, I think it would be nice if another exciting new Kiwi prospect emerged, and Gary could be the boy.

Physical knocks

He also started his British career up at Newcastle. He had a spell out on loan with Bradford in the second division, but was another one who showed that he could adapt to the increased pace and more sophisticated strategic requirements of the first division.

Peterson was all set to justify all the nice things that had been said about him last year when a family tragedy in New Zealand interrupted his progress. Just before Gary was due to come back for the British League season his sister was killed in a road accident. He had to stay home and thus 1972 was a year of no progress, racing wise.

But by the time I went back to New Zealand around Christmas, the kid was sorting himself out, riding again, and looking for all the world like another champion in the making. He has had some hard physical knocks as well, but keeps coming back. Probably, he has learned and will be that much wiser from now on.

Often, a rider goes well until he has had a bit of pain. That sorts the men from the boys. Some lose a little of their appetite and enthusiasm, but those who really want it come back, go on and don't let these things deflect them from their intended course.

Help and advice

I have been giving a bit of help and advice to a couple of English riders as well – Dave Jessup (Leicester) and my old mate Martin Ashby (Swindon).

Jessup is only 20, and yet rides with the quiet assurance of someone who has been around for many seasons. He was a member of the Kent Youth Motorcycle Association, which has done such a lot of good work in encouraging kids, so by the time he made his racing debut down at Eastbourne at 16 he knew plenty about riding a motorcycle.

From Eastbourne, to West Ham, Wembley and now Leicester, he showed increasing judgement and maturity. He is a cute little boy. Very sharp, knows the angles, totally different in approach from your Crumps, Petersons, or even Barry Thomas – the Hackney kid who started in similar fashion to Dave and must rate alongside him as just about the best of the crop of up and coming home products.

It still takes all sorts. Although the Olsen technique is something of a revolution in itself, there will still be others who prefer a more measured, leisured, and less spectaular approach. Jessup comes into that category. He is none the less effective, for all that.

What is good about him is his temperament, really terrific for a young boy. He doesn't flap or fluster, gets himself prepared and organised. And he showed that he wanted to get on and learn by going out to Rhodesia when the sport started up there again a couple of years ago. Nobody knew what the scene would be, but Jessup reckoned that whatever it was like, it would all be experience. So it was.

Maybe the standard of competition was not as high as if he had done a similar trip to Australia, but the basic lessons to be learned – about himself – were very similar.

The American invasion of British speedway really got underway in 1973 when Sumner McKnight (left) joined Swindon, Rick Woods (centre) went to Newport and Scott Autrey made his bow with Exeter.

As for Martin, the interest is a little different. He is in his late twenties, which could be against him reaching the very top. But in years of racing with him at Swindon, I appreciated the fact that as far as ability went there are very few better boys in the country.

Unfortunately this is something which Crash has never really believed sufficiently. What's more, like some of the other riders I have talked about in other chapters, he was never as enthusiastic to experiment, practise or perfect new ideas as I think you need to be to make that final jump from being a very good good racer into a world class one.

Yet in the British League Riders championship final at Belle Vue last year, he showed what could be done. Mart only got into the meeting because I was injured, although I knew all along that if he went about it the right way he had as good a chance as anybody.

We really went to work in the week before the meeting. He concentrated on the fitness angle more than he had ever done, prepared himself mentally, had the bike for the job – and shocked a lot of people (but not me I think) by finishing second with fourteen points.

Actually ridden

If I'm not winning meetings myself it is nice to think that riders whom I am encouraging either in practical or actual terms are going to continue to do something along the lines that I would have been pleased to do myself.

That's not to say that I have completely and totally finished with speedway racing. The trouble with British League speedway however is that you have to be available and on call for something up to eight months in the year subject to the requirements and commitments of your team and fairly obviously after 21 seasons, this is something I now reckon I can do without.

Clearly you just can't bale out without feeling a wrench. Although there are so many bright youngsters coming up I feel part of the scene. I know all the boys. Those I haven't actually ridden against I have seen or read about or probably dealt with in the bike business.

Most of our real friends are connected with racing. Fortunately though as a result of touring around the world, racing on the Continent, in America or down under there are loads of other people who come into the same category. I'll still be seeing just about as much of them as before.

But for a while I have wanted to be able to pick and choose my meetings. The joys of motoring up to Glasgow or down to Exeter for a run of the mill League meeting in which anyone who goes through the card can only expect to earn maybe £50 is something I can do without.

Don't get me wrong. I am grateful for the good times and the good living. There are a lot of riders quite happy with their lot in British speedway, riders who have won quite a few races fewer than me but still reckon it provides them with a decent living standard. However, it must be stated that anybody who cleans up in England throughout the season isn't going to become a rich man. The Promoters are still the only people who really get fat out of speedway. Whatever they may say there is plenty of money coming into speedway but not enough of it going out to the blokes without whom there would be no such sport.

Contrast this state of affairs with a weekend trip to the Continent where you get guaranteed appearance money, and good money at that. But of course you have to prove your ability to justify this sort of cash but once you're in, you're in.

And when that happens, nobody wants the gravy train to stop. The answer is: be smart, get organised, be professional and always be prepared to have a go. Do that and the Continentals will love you, and so of course will the Promoters. They don't mind saying thank you in the way riders like best.

It's the same in the States, except on an even larger and grander scale. Maybe its because of the fact that I am rarity value, but every time I go over the other side the treatment dished out is invariably fantastic. The purses aren't bad either.

Good enough, in fact, for my Accountant to have spent the last four or five years telling me what an idiot I was to continue with British League racing when there were such fabulous pickings to be had in the U.S.

June and I have looked at the situation and long ago we decided that we didn't want to be committed

Barry Briggs with showjumper Harvey Smith (right) and 'World of Sport' host Dickie Davies . . . and the respective autobiographies of Briggs and Smith.

to regular State side appearances. In the first place its a style and pace of living which doesn't completely appeal to me. Secondly, there's the kids and their education to consider – and from those points of view, British is best.

No, I'll settle for doing a handful of selected meetings over there. I can earn good money . . . and I do mean earn. I wouldn't like to give the impression that all I wanted to do was Hollywood about over there for five minutes, collect the loot, and then come home laughing all the way back to Southampton.

The Yanks wouldn't stand for it anyway. But they do appreciate when a fellow is putting on a show and this is something I have worked hard at in my visits over there.

Now I can go there without worrying whether I've got to be in Sheffield or Swindon the following night for a League match; I can tie in with my Continental commitments, which remain fairly plentiful.

I'm still a sucker for racing motorcycles and thus my withdrawal from the British scene doesn't mean to say that Briggo is a name from yesteryear.

Knowing the value of good physical fitness and still being prepared to work at it, I can keep myself in shape. The aim and intention was to wrap up the British speedway career with a World championship in 1972 but things didn't work out quite like that.

However that's all history now. I just want to get on with such racing as I choose to do; if and when I feel like a rest I can take it without any quarms or problems. The mid-fifties was my time for revolution. Arriving in England in 1952, I spent two or three years learning what it was all about and it was probably on one of the Trevor Redmond organised New Zealand tours to South Africa that I started to put things together.

I decided that to win races a more aggressive attitude on track was needed. By that I meant that Briggo felt there were quicker and better ways of manoeuvring a speedway bike round the circuits than favoured by many of the current top riders.

In those days it was all white line stuff take it carefully round the turns and give her the gun on the straights. Even as a raw kid I'd reckoned that you might as well try and get round the corners quickly as well. By putting this into practise in South Africa first and then back in England in I think it was 1955, I managed to get myself going far better than at any stage in my career to that point.

That was the year I should have won my first World Championship. Peter Craven spoiled all that by springing a result which surprised everybody – himself included – and I had to wait another couple of years. But by that time I wasn't the only rider using the 'new' style.

It was a policy and philosophy which hasn't changed too much in the intervening years; but you never can tell who is going to be smart enough to come up with some entirely new technique.

After all, once upon a time it was thought that leg trailing was the thing. Then came the foot forward technique. The advent of the eso machine also made riding a whole lot easier for many of the boys and that could probably be put down as one of the sports most significant developments in recent season.

Progress of any sort is essential if the sport is not to stagnate. I can think of a few good reasons how speedway in this country could be improved – publicity, support, sponsorship are obvious angles The attitude of the people at the top, though, is all important.

As long as riders are prepared to invest a lot and as long as the public are happy and willing to come and see and support the sport then surely there should be more in it for the riders. There's too much of this idea that you've got to keep the natives in ignorance.

The more enlightened (and realistic) the Promoters become the better response they will get from British League riders. The boys aren't asking for money that isn't there, but a lot of them feel that they don't want to be fobbed off any more by a Promoter who thinks that giving you a fiver bonus is the height of generosity.

This is the age of the speedway Superstar. Take men like Olsen and Mauger. Their life style, their jet set programme of commitments around the world ensure this.

In many ways I can't help feeling it might have been an idea to have come onto the scene now rather than in 1952. Still, perhaps one shouldn't complain; the good times have outweighed the bad and that's everything.

RIGHT: Barry gives his eldest son Gary a few tips before he has a trial run round the Swindon track. Barry's other son, Tony, looks on. BELOW: Gary, riding one of Barry's 500cc Jawas, has his first taste of speedway.

Ronnie Moore . . . pictured in the
colours of New Zealand.

BRIGGS and MAUGER

Are the English riders different in their approach to speedway than the 'foreigners'

PEOPLE often ask me about the prospects for English speedway, but in many ways it's an impossible question. Standards here are improving all the time, but other countries are making almost equally big strides forward. Today England might have two or three really world class riders but unless they demonstrate their ability in all countries and under many differing conditions, they won't get their name into the record books.

To succeed in 1973 a racer has to have an international outlook: he has to be prepared to have a go in all conditions and often against other blokes who go about the whole business very differently. There are people in other countries who feel that British is best – which basically it is – and have amended their own approach and techniques accordingly. As they do this, it is clear evidence that more and more challengers for top honours will keep springing up.

Ole Olsen sparked off a tremendous new interest in Denmark when he won the world championship a couple of years ago. There is a swinging new scene in West Germany and surely there will be some really good boys from there before long. They have the technical ability and the thoroughness to throw up some important challengers.

Then in East Germany they have got some good boys, none better than the big, blond Hans Jurgen Fritz – a fabulous bloke and a great prospect.

There will be more, and in the next chapter I'll be examining what England has coming up to meet the challenge. For the minute, though, I thought we could examine the basically different approach of riders from the various speedway countries.

Having come over from New Zealand and struggled, I know what it's about. Even now the Kiwis and Aussies get to England and show the home-bred boys a thing or two when it comes to determination and steel. Travelling half way round

the world to demonstrate your skills at riding a motor cycle is a hazardous business. It is also costly.

Unless a kid is lucky enough to find an English promoter who is prepared to stake him with a fare he might have to save his hard-earned pennies for months on end to afford the trip. And even if, as happens a bit these days, the passage money is found for him it doesn't mean that he will be in Easy Street on arrival.

A British promoter will be tempted to give a commonwealth rider an extended run to see if he will come good and live up to his home reputation, but it can't go on indefinately. If he isn't producing the goods fairly quickly he can't complain about getting the elbow.

Yet arriving in a strange country, finding your way around, getting into the routine of racing three or four times a week, travelling up and down the country, and just getting organised, can be a test of a youngester's staying power.

But most of them pass the test. They don't all become instant Jack Youngs or Ronnie Moores although some of the promoters and public seem to expect every new kid to be a champion inside five minutes.

Perhaps they have been spoiled in the past. And even so, the track record of Aussie and New Zealand boys coming over is very good, basically. Part of it must be down to their attitude.

If you give up a secure job back home, leave your friends and family 12,000 miles away, and try to make it in England, you're really thrown on to your own resources. For a lot of the riders who come, it is their first real test as a man and it doesn't take long to learn to become self-reliant. That's probably the first stage in manufacturing the hard shell a bloke needs.

Some of the English boys knock the fact that a visitor gets more chances and more encouragement than they do . . . but that's rubbish. Any promising kid will get encouragement, and rides, if he shows

HUNGRY TO HIT THE TOP

Christer Lofqvist (left) of Poole and Hasse Holmqvist of Oxford . . . two of the Swedes who race regularly in Britain.

the right ingredients. And after all, if you were a promoter, wouldn't you be inclined to give plenty of encouragement and opportunity to a youngster who had thrown all his eggs into the one basket and aimed for speedway success? The English boys, or some of them, complain about hard times but it's a joke.

Of course it isn't easy getting started in speedway. It takes a lot of dough and very often a lot of trouble, hard knocks and plenty of discouraging moments. But that's the same for anybody and everybody. And at least the English lads can go home to their own place at night, sleep in a warm bed and be reasonably certain of their three square meals a day.

Ronnie Moore (right) and Christer Lofqvist in action for New Zealand and Sweden respectively.

But plenty of Kiwi and Aussie lads in my experience have arrived in England with little more than the clothes they stood up in and a motor cycle to ride . . . virtually everything else has gone on the cost of the trip into (for them) the unknown.

There are necessities for racing in England; maybe only an old van but some reliable transport is needed . . . and then there's spares and other things. Living in luxury is bottom of the list of priorities. Sure, everybody wants to make the game a paying proposition, and success brings rewards which inevitably include some of the material comforts. But for the first year or two at least, it's likely to be a tough haul.

It's no joke trying to make a name for yourself in one of the toughest and most demanding of all professional sports – especially if your home is the back of a van or a corner of a caravan shared with two or three others, and the nearest you get to Cordon Bleu cooking is the daily round of beans on toast.

No wonder, then, that a lot of colonial boys are prepared to grit their teeth and work hard at improving their standards. No wonder they will race like hell for a third place point when maybe an English boy will settle for cruising to the flag.

If you come from Down Under it's virtually impossible NOT to aim for England to make a name for yourself and test your skill and potential against the best in the world.

But how many of the English boys jib at the prospect of going to Glasgow, let alone uprooting and removing half way round the globe for seven months of the year? How many of them put themselves out to get on the foreign trips, or to do an Australian tour? All we hear is that it's too long, too tough, too hot, too far, too much bother.

Well, in my experience and opinion, nothing should be too much bother if you want to make it to the top. Try anything and everything was my motto and that's the best advice I could give to any lad who wanted to know what he should do to push himself ahead of the pack.

Where has the pioneering spirit gone? It's quite an irony, isn't it, that Australians and New Zealanders should show the way like this, but obviously it is no accident that so many of us have done well in England.

When Ronnie, Trevor Redmond, and the rest of us were making a name for ourselves over here it was a big adventure. No doubt the kids of today like Phil Crump, Gary Peterson and the rest of them enjoy it all to the full and have themselves great times just as we did in the early days.

But the English temperament is a bit different. Some of them would explain their attitude by calling it professionalism. But saving a few shillings instead of trying something new isn't professionalism. Settling for a safe second place instead of battling for first isn't professionalism. Moaning about the good deal everybody else is supposed to get and complaining that nobody loves them isn't professionalism.

There are so many English riders with tremendous ability that it is ridiculous how many of them fail to live up to their potential. And a lot of it is to do with the state of mind which has never been checked.

Then again, there's no substitute for ability in this or any other sport. And even the hardest worker, the most dogged trier won't scale the heights unless he has that ability.

The Russians have proved this. In a dozen years since they came into international speedway they have only thrown up two or three really world class racers: Igor Plechanov, who was twice runner-up in a World Final, was the best of the bunch and they haven't got near replacing him since he retired.

But they're keen, busy, determined, and thorough. Trouble is that they just don't concentrate on the right things. All this business about being drilled and disciplined is ideal, but until they spread their wings and went out into the world, the Soviet boys were marking time. They were merely settling their own (not too high) standards and beating one another.

You cannot teach an old dog new tricks and the best day's work the Russkies did was to decide that the old guard had to go. Now they have a bright, smart and streamlined squad coming up and one or two of their young boys have the makings.

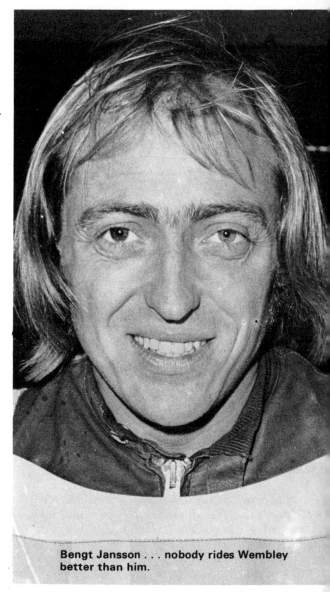

Bengt Jansson . . . nobody rides Wembley better than him.

When half a dozen Russians got through to Wembley in last year's World Final too many people tended to write them off and say that they would pose no threat. Yet some of them looked the part – in flashes at least. Antoli Kuzmin, who doesn't look much older than my Tony, is going to be a good little rider and Alexander Pavlov doesn't

27

look bad either. The elder Gordeev – Vladimir, the one banned for a year after being accused of using nitro in the Gothenburg Final of 1971 – could come back with a big bang, too.

They're still making the old mistakes, but their national style seems to be getting more mellow and smooth. That's experience. And the USSR authorities have put their boys about a bit in the last couple of years. The more they see of the way other countries are doing it, the more refined their naturally aggressive style becomes, the better their chances of getting someone near the big one.

The Poles have got a good crop of kids coming through as well. Their history has some parallels with the Russians, I suppose. They had some good racers, with Toni Woryna the best all-rounder, without quite conquering the world.

In the mid sixties it looked as if they were the coming force. They put it over us home and away but it amused me when the boys asked me to have a go although I'd been on the injured list. 'Come on Barry, we need you' they said . . . and this was only a few weeks after people had been saying, wasn't it good that we had got an ENGLISH team to face these foreigners!

Anyway, those Polskis had some good riders and a lot of people had a thing about them. Nobody fancied riding against them because very often they weren't too careful who or what they hit.

Eventually though we got over that and when a few of our boys got the bit between their teeth in the World Team Cup and showed the Poles that we'd had enough of it, the emphasis changed. The bogy has been well and truly laid now and oddly enough, it has probably caused the Poles to think again in their own international planning.

They really felt that they were the goods a few years ago, and with Edward Jancarz, only 20 then, coming on to the scene with a bang in the 1968 World Final, they were full of confidence.

A couple of year later, when Wroclaw was the stage for the first World Final in Poland, they were convinced that they could supply the world champion for the first time. Ivan put paid to all that, although Pawel Waloszek and Woryna grabbed second and third.

Waloszek has been a good racer but not quite that class. And he's another of the old guard, like Andrzej Pogorzelski, Andzej Wyglenda and Edmund Migos, good blokes all and good racers – in conditions which suited them. But coming to England found them out a few times.

Now the Poles, too, have set out on a policy to groom young riders and when they come up with kids like Jerzy Szczakiel and Zenon Plech, you'd better believe that they're on the right lines. The moral is that they have looked at their own weaknesses and set about to counter them.

In England we just go blithely along. I'm sad about that. Okay, so I've rubbished some of the attitudes and obviously it's good for New Zealand, particularly, if good kids come along.

At the same time, I have been connected with speedway in England since 1952; this is my home and whether people like to believe it or not, you can't represent Great Britain hundreds of times without caring a lot about it.

Therefore, I'm sorry that the potential of so many English boys is not properly brought out, although maybe it is starting to happen and if handled in the right way the situation can improve.

Maybe I regard myself as a bit of a hand when it comes to getting a bit extra out of the boys. Helping Martin Ashby when he got second place in the British League Riders' Final at Belle Vue last year was a case in point. But that wasn't my triumph – it was Mart's. At last he managed to realise what he could do and hopefully he also realised that you have to work at these things.

It isn't anywhere near enough to say: Okay, now I'll concentrate and take it seriously. You have to work at it. And for many boys, that would mean completely revising your attitudes, preparation and mental outlook before and during meetings.

If too many Englishmen don't do themselves justice, and if a high proportion of Aussies and New Zealanders have made the grade simply because of those attitudes, how about the Swedes? You can't argue with their phenomenal record of producing top riders – and that's probably down to their national trends of thought, too.

It is my impression that the average Swede is probably more selfish than you could say of a lot of racers. They put a high emphasis upon doing it their own way, they have achieved Europe's highest living standards because of a materialistic outlook . . . some of it must surely have rubbed off on quite a few of their riders. Take my old oppo Fundin. There's no doubt Ove was a great racer, a terrific competitor and opponent. Nobody could call him Mister Popularity though. Basically all he was interested in was himself.

Everybody got used to Ove's scenes and tantrums down the years but he was smart with it. And when the chips were down, he would be so ice cool and detached, concentrating only on winning the vital race.

I've had many a run-in with Fundin. The battles we had! There again, for ten years or so he wanted to prove to all and sundry that he was the world's best. And that was bound to lead to some friction and one or two clashes.

Bjorn Knutsson was different – a great mate of mine, especially when we rode together at Southampton. And we've remained good friends ever since.

Even so, Knutty could be so sharp and steel and he didn't know any fear. When the handicapping system was used in 1963 and 1964 – originally it applied to Fundin, Peter Craven, Ronnie, Bjorn and myself – he was the one who beat it best of all. In fact it probably made him an even better rider: all the rest of us had been the world's champion but he was still trying and it wasn't before time when he made it in 1965.

Impeccable manners

Gote Nordin, who goes down as the best rider of recent years not to win the world title, was what I'd call the typical Swede. Everybody knows him as a charming bloke, with impeccable manners and that cool Scandinavian look of groomed confidence. When he rode regularly in England he had a tremendous following and was a great pin-up and favourite.

But beneath it all, and out on the track where it mattered, Gote was the hardest rider imaginable. He would think nothing of putting it across you and certainly he wasn't as well loved by the riders as by the watchers for whom he could do no wrong.

Bengt Jansson is another 'near miss' man who has been second and third in World Finals but seems to fall just short of the big one. People put this down to the fact that Banger is just too nice a guy but he can react when the heat is on.

When he first came over to West Ham in 1964 he did nothing at the start. They were all set to send him back to Sweden, but Bjorn had a word in his ear and Jansson didn't waste any time after that.

Straight confrontation

I couldn't believe it when Banger went out of the world championship at the European Final stage last year. Apparently he had some diabolically bad luck in Poland and some of the misfortunes which hit him shouldn't happen to a dog. The funny – or sad – part about it was that nobody rides Wembley better than Jansson.

Soren Sjosten missed out as well which was a rare failure for Manchester's good littl'un and most of the Swedish hopes centred around Anders Michanek. Now there's another bloke to illustrate my point. Mich is okay when everything is going well for him and he's one of the best riders around, but it all has to be just right. He isn't such good company when things are going badly.

As it turned out, it was Bernt Persson who almost caused a surprise and took Ivan Mauger to a run-off for first place. There was no way he would have beaten Ivan in a straight confrontation like that, but still it showed that he has a terrific chance.

Little Christer Lofqvist, too, is another good prospect. He can be spectacular, brilliant, or just plain unpredictable but there are signs that he's getting himself built up for another go. He is a great Fundin admirer and state of mind is all important to Christer. That's what it's all about.

The big thing is ability, though. You cannot hope to be a world class rider unless the ability is there. Garry Middleton, the noisiest Aussie of them all, could come through. I always reckoned he had a bit of class. His basic style needs sharpening up but there's something there.

Psychologically though, he's a puzzle, a real Jekyll and Hyde. He has had a lot of good ideas but too many bad ones and if he is going to make the top he just might have to listen to somebody else's advice.

But you can't knock the boy for trying. He pulled himself up because he had the hunger – which is just about where we came in.

Barry Briggs displays his skill at ten-pin bowling . . . but are leathers and Southampton race-jacket really the gear for this particular sport? Barry, of course, was with the Southampton speedway team until the track closed in 1964.

BELOW: Briggo leads Rick Woods of America in a charity meeting at the Santa Barbara track in California. Money raised at this meeting helped pay for the lights at the local football stadium.

A champion's guide to what speedway riders should wear: strong boots, a reliable steel-show strap and plenty of support round the ankles – note the elastic bands! Who's the model? Think about it. The answer can be found on page 110.

ENGLAND EXPECTS..

Barry looks at the boys who carry British hopes in the international arena

HAVING said my say about the deficiencies and shortcomings of too many English riders, how about those who carry the country's international hopes? I'll happily admit that the picture is not totally black. And I feel sure that if a lot of these boys were pointed in the right direction they could do much better for themselves.

John Louis, whom we discussed earlier, is an example to the rest of the boys. His attitude is right. He has this burning desire to do well, and this was reflected both at a personal level and when he rode in the World Final and World Team Cup.

This nationalistic spirit is probably easier to cultivate if you're from overseas and racing in a foreign country. In this respect it's been easier, say, for Ivan and me. We have had to battle from the start, especially on the continent where very often you have to change in a field, race in conditions which leave plenty to be desired, and bath in a local hotel.

Hardship, though, is part of getting into the groove to be a winner. Boys who tackle the continent are going about things the right way. Louis did this. So did little Dave Jessup, who at 20 must be one of England's best hopes. I like Jessup's approach. He is always eager, presentable, and gives everything. There was one meeting in Germany where he'd been given the wrong information and turned up for a long track with just a standard speedway bike . . . yet he was always in amongst it.

In the Laurels at Wimbledon towards the end of the season he came so close to pulling off one of the major titles of the season. He reacts so well even under pressure. Ivan and I were rooting for him to be taken to Olching on the World Team Cup trip . . . even if he didn't ride the experience would have been good for him. He didn't make that one but there isn't much doubt that he will be on a few in the next year or two.

Jessup started riding a motor cycle when he was just a little kid and he first came to public notice with Barry Thomas. They were the star members of the Kent Youth Motor Cycle Association and Dave Lanning put them in some exhibition events at West Ham. Even then the youngsters showed remarkable maturity, and it illustrates the fact that you cannot start the kids too young. There are quite a few of these youth motor cycle clubs around the place and basically they are doing a good job.

Barry Thomas . . . an English lad with tremendous potential. Rides for Hackney.

My boys both ride and irrespective of whether they – or any of the other youngsters who ride – go on to become professional racers, the set-up teaches them to respect motor cycling, to treat their machinery properly and not to take any liberties.

The motor cyclist has a bad image even now, because there are some irresponsible clowns who like to Hollywood-about on the roads. But the average motor cyclist is sane and sensible, and the right sort of people are schooling these young boys in the proper way. This obviously happened with Jessup, and with the string of other boys from that area who have since come into speedway.

But it's still fun and Thomas is a boy who hasn't forgotten that. In so many ways he reminds me of myself at the same age and stage of development. He is a big, strong and determined rider and although he hasn't achieved consistency yet, he has

done enough to warn all the big stars that he is going to be a coming force in the not too distant future.

He has been to Australia with the British Lions and that won't have done him any harm at all. He could have gone in 1971 but possibly unwise advice persuaded him to turn down the trip. Barry can ride really fabulous and among the young boys he has possibly got the greatest potential. He has confidence and as long as he is prepared to heed one or two lessons he should come good in a big, big way.

It can take some riders a long time to see the light, though. Terry Betts, technically, must be one of the top Englishmen and he's still young enough to get better. He had a very good year in 1972 and a lot of it was down to a different attitude.

In the past Bettsy was always something of a joke among the boys. He always had this great ability but he'd tend to be slap-happy in some of his attitudes and this undoubtedly held him back. He was good enough to beat anybody if the mood was on him but simply you just never knew what he was going to do.

Probably he wasn't as meticulous with his equipment as some of the boys and however much talent a rider has, he cannot expect to beat top class rivals unless he's at least on a par mechanically. I wouldn't have called him the greatest 'organisation' man either, although no doubt some of my closest friends would call that a case of the pot calling the kettle black!

With all this I suppose Terry commanded a lot of respect on the quiet – simply because in spite of all these habits he still went on getting good results and earning – and justifying – international selection and so on.

But in 1972 it was a different Bettsy. He was so much more organised and thorough. He spent more time on his equipment, experimented in situations where before he would probably have left well alone, and although he was still the same sunny personality he's always been, deep down you knew that he'd added a tougher streak.

I had some early evidence of that at the beginning of the season when Swindon went up to King's Lynn and we had a run-in on the track. The referee

Dave Jessup of Leicester and England. Also one of the 'Briggo Boys'.

xcluded me but it was Terry's fault . . . and in another year he would probably have admitted as much and asked the referee to put me back in the race. Not this time.

Now normally Terry is the sort of bloke you like racing with. He's fast and he's fair. You end up thinking that you won't bother to move him over whereas if it's somebody you don't rate as a person there is no hesitation about getting stuck in. That's soft thinking, though, because when it comes down to it nobody is your mate out there on the track. I made a mistake that time but it's one I wouldn't repeat.

Terry is still a good, fair and honest bloke but last year was that much better for him because he decided to save his nice guy act for off the track. You don't have to be dirty to win races and in this game the fellow who does diabolical tricks is liable to get sorted out; but there is a world of difference between that and just adding that extra steel.

Now that he had included this in his make-up, you could see Bettsy getting better still. I'd like to see it. The boy is always good value and riders and fans alike wouldn't begrudge him a taste of the really big success.

Ray Wilson is another keen and ambitious rider. I'm still not quite sure about him, though. He can reel off two or three really terrific races against riders of the highest quality, but there is a question mark against his ability to do it throughout a meeting.

In the World Team Cup meeting in Poland in 1971 he got a colossal maximum. He looked a world champion. Then he had a diabolical clang in the second half event and it all seemed so senseless. Maybe he'd got a bit carried away with what had gone before. But this is something you cannot do if you want to strike gold.

Ray is a boy who I'd like to see do really well because he never made any secret of the fact that he reckoned my way of doing things. Apparently when he was a kid at Leicester he used to regard me as his favourite rider and naturally if anybody decides to try to emulate you it's nice if they come good.

Wilson cannot complain because he's been a big scorer in League matches, consistent in internationals, and impressive against all the best of them in a number of open meetings. But there's always that unpredictability about him. And if

Terry Betts of Kings Lynn

anybody cares to look at the list of riders who have dominated at the top in the last 20 years, they will see that those who make the final step don't have many bad meetings.

Ray still has it in him to have the occasional ghastly night and he doesn't always rationalise when things go wrong. He goes at it rather like a bull in a china shop, and while you can't doubt his determination or enthusiasm there's more needed than that. At the same time, it is a tribute to him in a way that one has come to judge him only by the highest standards. He's done enough at domestic level to be thought of

as something better even than the best club performers.

Eric Boocock is another puzzle. He has a style which suits at certain places. See him go round Exeter and he looks like a world champion. Other times he disappoints. In so many respects Eric is an example to speedway riders. He spends hours on his bikes, is always neat in appearance and these pointers count for a lot.

But maybe, like elder brother Nigel, he has something missing from his make-up and although a regular World Final qualifier and all that sort of thing, he falls just a step or two short.

There's a pile of riders who come into or approach that category. Arnold Haley of Sheffield, very brisk and brave, Trevor Hedge – a good rider but never confident enough of his own ability – and Bob Kilby are three who spring to mind. But why don't they bridge the gap between doing well at League level and making a big show in the international sphere? There could be 1001 reasons in each case.

Then look at Martin Ashby, who might be as good an English rider as anybody if he was more decisive. We demonstrated last October that Martin can beat anybody. People have asked me just what I did him to make so much difference to his performanc at Belle Vue. It wasn't too much, but it added up

We've had many talks down the years abou attitude, preparation and so on. I'm a physica fitness fanatic, and have always believed in th importance of keeping myself sharp. Martin rathe tended to dismiss all this. But . . . he gave up smoking channelled his thoughts in the right direction, go himself in the right shape for the meeting.

He got himself properly organised, studied ever detail of the track, every one of his opponents, an began to realise that he had nothing to fear from an of these blokes. Okay, so this was the gathering o the 16 top scorers, the number one man from eac First Division track. So what? He had beaten then all at some time or another. And he could bet tha some of them would beat themselves on this big night

He'd done it himself often enough – and once bloke decides that he isn't quite good enough or the circumstances aren't just right he might as well pack up and go home. But this time he simply went ou and rode forcefully, aggressively and like the very polished racer he is.

Martin Ashby of Swindon.

Some people have tended to under-rate Martin down the years, perhaps just because he was used to being regarded as second best to me at Swindon and therefore, by definition, second best at any time. Little did they know that his tremendous form, especially round Blunsdon, was always a factor in keeping me on the mark; he was good for me in the same way that Bjorn Knutsson had been at Southampton when each was always trying to beat the other.

Yet for all that Ashby tended to believe what other people thought and it was a mistake which held him back for years. Whether he can sustain a high level of really positive thinking in his approach remains to be seen. But his Belle Vue display was his success after all. I couldn't do a thing for him once he sat on the bike and it underlines what I've said about riders not realising their potential.

Jimmy McMillan, the best of the Scottish boys, is another very good boy who was promised a lot. He may yet achieve something better, but he too has probably suffered from being under-rated and ending up by believing it himself.

As much because of his geographical situation as anything else, Jimmy hasn't had so many open bookings and big meetings as his talent warrants. At first you can put it down to the fact that there are equally good riders more easily available. In the end the thought that he would get asked down if he was really good enough, but not otherwise, must have made him doubt his own capabilities.

If ability was the only criterion you would expect Malcolm Simmons to have come to the fore by now. He's a natural, one of the best all-round motor cyclists of recent years. Malcolm was a national grass track champion at 17 and he has a good style which adapted easily to speedway. Ken McKinlay taught him a lot at West Ham a few years ago and at times Malcolm looks so full of class.

But he is another of this legion of very good riders who don't seem able to make that final jump. He's young enough to do it, though.

The most likely prospect of them all, however, could be this boy Peter Collins up at Belle Vue. He is another of the grass track graduates, like Chris Pusey before him. I haven't seen all that much of

**One of England's best prospects . . .
Peter Collins of Belle Vue.**

Barry Briggs with Graeme Stapleton of Wimbledon.

Collins but what I have seen has been impressive. He is another cool customer, who pays attention to detail, doesn't flap and he certainly can ride a motor cycle.

Knockers have said that he relies too much upon a sponser who holds his hand and does everything for him, but good luck to the boy. Fundin didn't want to know a thing about his motor cycle, except to be damn sure that it went quickly and reliably.

The Collins bikes do that and more, and he knows where to point them. And going to Australia will certainly have made him a whole lot more self-reliant. It's no bad idea to be clued up on the subject even if the donkey work is done by others.

I have got some of the best experts working on my motor cycles. Brother Murray knows them inside out and there are others whose names might not be so familiar with the general public but know all that's worth knowing on the subject. But I still like to be able to do it myself if need be, to understand what is required and to be able to do it.

It's as much a matter of time and expediency as anything else that I leave so much of it to the boys. It would be impossible to find enough hours in the day to do everything.

It's vital to get one's priorities right, though. I have the business to consider, and almost all of the English riders have some other sideline to think about.

When racing, however, business interests and all the rest of it has to be relegated to a proper place in the queue. After all, it's probable that any business interests have been started as a result of, or as a direct link with, racing a motor cycle . . . successfully.

This English idea that the sport pays well enough and that if you don't win every race today, there's always another meeting tomorrow – it's been bad for British speedway. Winning is vitally important and unless riders develop an attitude of mind whereby every defeat hurts, they won't scale the greatest heights.

Everybody likes to win, but for a lot of people it's a bonus. But to, say, John Louis, it's important to win every time. Now to some people that is all wrong. I don't agree. If some folk are sensitive about it, maybe John should play down the fact that this is what he wants . . . but then again, why should he?

The Corinthian attitude might have been fine in 1873 but we've progressed some since then.
I hope.

Ray Wilson . . . a fine action shot of the England and Leicester captain.

Down Memory La

TOP LEFT: The Great Britain team before their match against the Soviet Union at Wolverhampton in 1968. Left to right: Charles Ochiltree (manager), Barry Briggs, Eric Boocock, Nigel Boocock, Martin Ashby, Ivan Mauger, Jim Airey, Ken McKinlay and Peter Vandenberg. TOP RIGHT: Ron Johnson (left) and Ronnie Moore pictured at Belle Vue. BOTTOM LEFT: Former Wimbledon favourite Ernie Roccio, killed at West Ham in 1952.

he

CENTRE: That great Kiwi character Bruce Abernathy — Briggo got him out of retirement in New Zealand earlier this year. 'I was once his pusher,' says Barry. 'Now he oiled and fuelled for me!' RIGHT: Barry, with brother Wayne at Wolverhampton.

WEMB

WEMBLEY, 1972, was going to be the
grand finale – the spectacular fare-
well. I had more or less made up my
mind months before the World Final that this
would be my last year as a full-time racer. And
there was one thing I needed before giving
away the speedway game . . . a fifth world's
championship.

You might think that, with four, I would be
satified. But as long as you go on racing, you're
never satisfied. There is no point in going on unless
there is a very real chance of being the top dog once
again. Down the years I developed an appetite for
winning. I never felt the same about coming second.

When you have been in the game for a number of
years, it is always so difficult to know which is the
right moment to give it away. I love riding motor
cycles and even after twenty years I still enjoy
competition. But that has been because I have
always been able to compete at the highest level.

It was always a matter of pride that if and when
the day arrived when clearly I couldn't stay with
the boys, that would be the time to say: enough. It's
all a matter of timing, and it is a natural wish that
you can quit while still at the top.

I hadn't won a world title since 1966, but I still
considered myself fully capable of doing so. There
are always 1001 reasons why one doesn't do something, but I had chances to have won at least a
couple more championships. Probably in recent
years I have been silly to myself. Apart from racing
flat out in Britain and Europe, there's been the
JAWA business to worry about. Since most of the
British boys starting using the ESO, it has boosted
my business and bank balance and also contributed
a few grey hairs.

The boys who complain if stocks are in short
supply or that they cannot get spares when they
want them should take a rest cure of a month trying
to run the business. Then perhaps they would see,
understand and appreciate the sort of effort which
goes in to trying to provide them with a really good
service. By and large we don't do a bad job but there
are times when nothing goes right.

Dealing with Czechoslovakia is a whole problem
in itself and often the only way to sort out delivery
dates or to guarantee that the next shipment is
coming is to belt out there to see for yourself. The
factory goes along at its own regulated pace and
sometimes even personal intervention can't do
anything to speed up supplies. But you have to try.

This involves charging about, visiting various
embassies, getting visas and documents, driving half
way round Europe, catching ferries, chatting up
border officials . . . it's some enterprise. Trying to do
all this, plus fitting in racing commitments which,
until I took the decision to quit the British League,
meant spending at least 36 hours of each day
worrying about bikes, travel and all the rest of it, is
bound to take its toll.

If my programme had been less cluttered, my
schedule more streamlined, there isn't a lot of
doubt that my speedway performances over the past
few seasons could have been that much better.

If you want to consult the record books you will
see that the figures are quite impressive anyway,
that even after 1966 I was still up there, in the top
two or three in the world rankings. But with a little
more organisation maybe I could have taken another
title or two. In 1969, for example, I felt so ripe and
ready for another championship. There was no way
I was going to fail. But I did, and Ivan Mauger
collected his second successive title that year.

You can't take anything away from Mauger, or
Ove Fundin, who has the record of five world
championship wins. There they are, in the record
books. But within myself, I never wanted to be
second best to any of them. Blokes who have been
friends and/or rivals . . . it makes no difference. It's
still something personal about wanting to beat them.

I didn't expect to top Fundin's five titles but when
1972 came around and I decided that the fooling had
to stop, I set my mind on winding up with just one
more championship to level the score. More than

EY '72

a year that began with high hopes and ended ➡

Barry Briggs talking to Dickie Davies on the ITV 'World of Sport' programme. It was here that Briggo announced his decision to retire from British League racing.

Diligent attention for a Briggo machine from Stan Palmer (left), Murray Briggs (centre) and Jimmy Gallacher.

anything it was a case of getting my own record straight. I knew I could still race with the best of them. Maybe there were some riders, some fans, some officials even, who thought I was over the top.

But you can be honest with yourself. I knew that it looked that way. But I also knew that a world championship was still there for the taking, still within my grasp.

Even after all these years, who else was there? Mauger, terrific starter, tremendous concentration and professionalism, a real champion. But much as I admired Ivan, I didn't ever worry about having to race against him. Olsen, the 1971 champion and clearly the coming force, so fast and yet still prone to do the ridiculous and throw away everything with one lunatic mistake.

And after these two, you couldn't see another rider in the world capable of putting together five consistent rides on Final night. Sometimes freaks occur but as often as not, anybody with ambitions about winning the championship simply has to have the ability to put together five perfect rides. Four good ones and one disaster won't win the big one.

Fitness-wise, everything was still good with me. It's no accident. Physical well-being has always been a matter of tremendous importance and although a lot of the boys have rubbished me because I go running, swimming and all that sort of stuff, it's kept me sharp.

I don't believe in spoiling my physical fitness with smoking or drinking. I like my food but being a big fellow for a racer I have to watch it. If it wasn't for working at my fitness, I expect it would be easy to

44

out on weight . . . but training has never been a hardship. In other words, even though I was giving a year or two to some of my opponents, I wasn't giving them a thing where fitness was concerned.

Who can say when the time comes that reactions start to go? I can honestly say that I don't know the answer to that one . . . but by maintaining peak physical fitness I have kept myself in shape and it would be easy to let it go otherwise. So, from these angles, there was nothing to worry about. It was largely a matter of organisation, preparation, mental awareness and, of course, getting a bike to go.

In 1971 I had so much trouble it wasn't true. So many things went wrong with my bikes that it was a bad year for me, so bad, in fact, that I vowed to give it away if I ever had that amount of trouble again. I didn't imagine that I could have so much bother, but 1972 proved that wrong, as events turned out.

Before the start, though, all was optimism. Good blokes work on my bikes: brother Murray, Roy Forfitt and people like this know what they are doing. I've got a fair idea myself. Once upon a time, when I was young and foolish, I was known as the string and wire man but even then the jokes didn't disguise the fact that my motor cycles still went as quickly as anybody else's and faster than most.

So I felt well set up. Even more than this, the old publicity machine was turning again. It's no accident how this happens. During the winter of 1971–72 we were setting up my book 'Briggo' and clearly it would have been a bad deal if the public were not reminded of my existence.

This meant a fairly concerted publicity build-up, and I didn't mind letting the world know that I meant business in 1972. Probably I had been too quiet, too pre-occupied with my own problems, to keep pushing my image in the preceding few years. Back around the time I won those two world titles in Sweden, there was a load of publicity, and Keith Goodwin helped tremendously with all that. The television coverage and all that sort of stuff didn't do any harm, either.

But I had got busier, and so had Keith, so things went quiet for a while. Now it was beginning to build up again. A lot of stuff you read can be forgotten in a minute. But, like anybody else, I don't mind people writing nice things about me. To pick up a newspaper or magazine which stated in black and white the thoughts I was cultivating in my own mind was like confirmation that I really meant it.

Trouble was that in the first couple of months of the 1972 season, things backfired. I was constantly getting the dirty end of the stick. One or two decisions went against me in meetings which were nothing in themselves, yet it was annoying. Even more niggling was the worry about getting a bike to go.

All sorts of jinxes pursued me. My speedway machine misbehaved for no reason. I could go out, test the thing for three hours and end up convinced that it was perfect. Then it would pack up at a meeting. It gave up on me on the stand when being warmed up before a world championship meeting at Exeter.

It was no better on the continent. I had terrible trouble on some of those trips. That's all you need – dashing around, driving or flying a thousand miles and then have the bike play up. But it wasn't just me. I even borrow bikes from people like Ivan and Sture Lindblom and they fell to pieces, too. Things went wrong that you wouldn't believe.

It was frustrating to say the least. You key yourself up to do well, it's a necessary part of getting to the pitch at which you can go out and blow off all opposition. But then the big let-down as one snag after another cropped up.

In between times I was winning some but all the time in the back of my mind was the nagging worry . . . what was going to go wrong next? It's impossible to concentrate on racing when this sort of run is upon you. My nerves began to fray at the ends, and it was bad for Junie and the kids, too. When it gets so bad that they suffer it really is time to think about jacking it in.

The Wills International at Wimbledon on Whit Monday was the last straw. We had spent all day Sunday practising and testing at Weymouth. That sort of extra exercise I needed like a hole in the head. But at least at the end of it I was satisfied that everything was right and ready for one of the first big speedway meetings of the year in England.

Everybody would be there – Mauger, Olsen, all the boys. It's always a good meeting, a big crowd and TV covering the whole show. It couldn't be better. A good performance would be a big morale booster. I didn't get it because once again the bike turned out to be useless. And against that sort of opposition you can do without all the battling. You want the bike to be right and then it's just a question of dealing with the challenge of 15 other riders, all of whom are in and around world class.

I was so disgusted and I wasn't going to put up with looking like a clown in that company or in front of a big crowd. I finished the meeting but had already decided that there was only one thing for it . . . a break from racing, a spell away from everything and everyone. The pressure had built up and built up and that night it was just too much.

I don't know what I thought. For two pins I was ready to give it away there and then, but on reflection it seemed pointless to go out like that. I was still in the championship and, in the back of my mind, sick though I was at the time, I knew that Wembley was the goal.

At Plough Lane that night, though, I'd had it. I simply needed to get away, get out. Some newspapermen got hold of the story that I had quit, retired completely. We had to issue a quick denial on that one. A couple of close mates in the writing game knew what the scene was and at least they knew as much about it as I did myself. I explained that ten days or a fortnight away from it all could do a lot to sort me out.

I spent a couple of days at the office, tying up a few loose ends, and then Junie, Gary and Tony and I flew off to Spain. We've got a place there. Sun and sea proved to be a great tonic. From being wound up like an alarm clock, I gradually managed to come down.

It was tough for Junie. She knew how much '72 was supposed to mean. She also knew that it's quite a knife-edge between deciding to go on and sticking with it. As always, though, she knew that I had to reach the decision and whichever way it went, she would back me up.

Anyway, after collecting a tan, taking some rest which was just what the doctor ordered, I decided to get back with the action. The first meeting back was another stern test, the Silver Plume individual meeting at Swindon. It would have been good to get back by winning that one, because once again Ivan, Ole and the rest of them were all there.

As it turned out, Ray Wilson beat me at the death but at least I had got 14 points out of 15 and

although the bike wasn't good, it didn't stop either. That made a change.

I thought that I could re-adjust, get myself back in the groove. I picked through the world championship semi-finals at Leicester without too much bother. And there were some New Zealand test matches coming up to provide variety. But one of those – at Belle Vue – brought more bother. There was a giant prang with John Langfield, just one of those things which happen, and boy, was I lucky to crawl out of it.

Folk reckoned it was the most spectacular and dodgy-looking crash they had ever seen at Manchester. I ripped up a twenty yard section of the safety fence and did myself no good at all. Yet once again it was the fact that by great physical condition saved me from a lot more damage. If I had been anything less than full of health, partly with the usual training routine and partially I suppose after that break, then boy it could have been a whole heap more troublesome.

As it was it kept me out of the saddle for another two or three weeks, just at a time when I needed to race. The British Final at Coventry was coming up and I needed to be one of the top five to qualify for that Wembley date. In the event, I managed to get back in time, and sure enough qualified at Brandon. It wasn't a Briggo super show or anything like that, but after all the dramas I was far more concerned about getting through in one piece, with the bike not stopping and with enough points to qualify. Winning the meeting didn't mean a thing.

Now there were six weeks to wait before the World Final itself. One diversion in the intervening period was our haggle with the promoters for more money. Advance bookings were high and all the indications were that this was going to be the richest pay-night ever in speedway . . . for everybody except the boys.

The way we reckoned it, what with an estimated 80,000 spectators paying good money, programme and other sales, TV rights and all the rest of it, the cash situation needed urgent review. The winner was in for £1,000 but the chances were that anybody who filled one of the lesser placings would go home with less than he might do from an ordinary run-of-the-mill League match.

Yet with so much public interest and so much cash flying about, it seemed all wrong that the boys shouldn't get a hand on any of it. After all, the ticket sales from the tracks alone amounted to thousands of pounds. Even allowing for the annual share-out to tracks, which is an important part of helping to subsidise the sport, it was clear that the distribution was cock-eyed. There are promoters who treat the boys well and there are those who drive around in their limousines yet plead poverty.

Anyway, the Wembley qualifiers – Ivan, the Boocock brothers, John Louis and reserve Jim McMillan – and myself made representations for more money, just so that we could get some appearance money at least to make all the championship effort worthwhile.

After all, to prepare for the big night isn't just a matter of spending half an hour in the workshops tinkering with the bike. It's a long, arduous, demanding build-up and you might spend hundreds on bits and pieces to get the thing set up right.

There were various wild tales circulating about what we had asked for, and more stories about what we would do if our demands were not met. All great publicity! Eventually, after various meetings, arguments, going back and forth, the affair was brushed aside and we all got down to the business of concentrating upon the real task in hand.

It was a distraction we could have done without. Still, if the others wanted to let the issue over-ride other considerations, that was up to them. For me, it was time to get really into the groove for the big night. After weeks of painstaking and exhaustive work we managed to get one machine going sweetly.

We had built up a new bike, with a standard JAWA engine. One of the not-so-standard features about the bike was its weight. It was a real light-weight. Years before I had built a special light machine and been pleased with the results. It seemed like a good idea to do so again. I'm a couple of stone heavier than people like Ivan and Louis; this was one way of getting parity. And the power to weight ratio is an important factor at starts. The Wembley Special was kept under wraps except for specific occasions but she was a smooth one.

In fact the whole prelude seemed right. It was as good as at any time since 1964 when I had a terrific run and could do no wrong. There was no way I could get beaten in Gothenburg that year and the way it was shaping I was beginning to feel really confident about Wembley '72.

A moment of despair for Briggo, at the 1972 Wills Internationale after engine failure had caused him to pull out of a race.

You get the feeling and a few good results, both on the continent and in England, confirmed the thoughts. It had been a topsy-turvey year, those traumas early on, injury, and all the rest of it. But now I was feeling sharp again. There was a bit of trouble with the knee which had been hurt at Manchester, but that was nothing that couldn't be coped with.

Olsen and Mauger were still the obvious favourites. But for the moment it didn't matter

47

whether anybody else rated my chances or not. I was rating them and that was what counted. At the practice two days before the Final everything was perfect. I did what I needed to do, proved everything to my own satisfaction, clowned around a bit, learned a great deal about the track, and felt like a million dollars.

For a spell I sat up in the roof at Wembley, gazing down on the track learned a great deal about its shape, realised things that had baffled me while actually down there riding. A long chat with Ronnie Moore also revealed a great deal.

The first few copies of 'Briggo' were in the back seat of the car. Business partner Phil Rising said: 'Keep this up and we might sell a few on Saturday night.' In my heart I felt that this was the final chapter and I have this thing about happy endings. It was almost certain that this was going to be my last World Final appearance and I was convinced that I could go out with just the right flourish . . . another championship win.

I told David Hamilton as much when we chatted on BBC Radio's 'Late Night Extra' on the Friday before the Final. And David, who also wanted to chat about the newly-published autobiography, asked me about the injury aspect of speedway racing. I told him that it's something you have to be philosophical about.

Little did I know that less than 24 hours later those dreams of bowing out with a Wembley win were finished – and a second race crash cost me the index finger of my left hand.

Yet the evening couldn't have begun better. I was confident, so much so that I wore a pair of driving gloves instead of the usual racing ones. Bjorn Knutsson, who came along to help if necessary, suggested I change. 'What if you get behind?' he asked. But the thought of being behind, for very long anyway, never really crossed my mind. Out front was where I was going to be.

The crowd seemed to sense it, too. It is an unbelievable sensation, when you feel that something

World Champion Ivan Mauger . . . Briggo writes about his New Zealand colleague later in this book.

Briggo's first competitive motorcycle event after the Wembley crash . . . riding a trials event in Dorset.

is going to happen and at the same time 75,000 people appear to get the same idea. I blew off Ivan in my first race and it all seemed just right: the bike, me, the occasion.

But after ditching Mauger, and with Olsen ruefully contemplating the thought that he had spilled his chances by falling off in his first ride, it was wide open for me.

Then came the second race, the buffeting with Persson, the collision course of two Russians who used me as a launching pad . . . an accident which has been shown and reshown so many times on television that it must be just about the most used scrap of speedway action ever filmed.

The upshot of it all was a trip to hospital, removal next day to Mount Vernon, Northwood, where specialists examined the index finger and said that it was so badly damaged that I would be better off without it. Sure, it was a nasty accident, but these

things happen. It needn't have happened, but it isn't much use crying about it now.

It could have been much worse. I'm hardly affected really and there certainly wasn't any question that the injury was the reason for announcing my decision to retire from the British League . . . a decision already 90% formulated before Wembley, and turned into fact when I appeared with Dickie Davies on ITV's 'World of Sport' and announced my retirement.

Even now I'm sad that the last Wembley show couldn't have been capped by that title I wanted so much. I'm sad because it was there for the taking and I lost it, not through any fault of my own. If it had been my own stupid fault it would have been that much easier to take.

Still, no time for regrets. Wembley '72 turned out to be special . . . but not quite in the way intended. That's the way it goes.

49

Briggo in New Zealand

TOP LEFT: Briggo in a Ford Anglia saloon before driving in a novelty race against Ronnie Moore and Ivan Mauger at Gisborne. BOTTOM LEFT: Briggo playfully aims his mini-bike at a Speedway Racing News photographer after deciding not to go up the ramp. TOP RIGHT: Briggs, Moore and Mauger before a radio interview in Hasting at the N.Z.B.C. studio. BOTTOM RIGHT: Champions' wives — left to right Jill Moore, June Briggs and Raye Mauger.

Remember Southampton ?

TOP LEFT: Barry Briggs of Southampton pictured at Bannister Court. BOTTOM LEFT: Briggo leads Ove Fundin of Norwich in a British Match Race Championship heat at Southampton. TOP RIGHT: This time Ove Fundin leads Bjorn Knutsson in another Match Race Championship. BOTTOM LEFT: The inimitable, late Peter Craven in a World Championship round at Bannister Court.

RIGHT Manfred Poschenreider illustrates that it doesn't always pay to look where you're going. BELOW LEFT: In another superb picture, Poschenreider again seems to say 'I can't look!' BELOW RIGHT: Another technique from an unnamed rider — he simply shuts his eyes!

'I can't look!'

Barry Briggs gives some advice to 19-year-old Scott Autrey, who came to England from America this season to ride for Exeter.

The Briggs family . . . Barry, June, Gary (with ball) and their alsatian dog, Lady.

MARRIED TO A TOP RACER

by
JUNE BRIGGS

Life as the wife of a professional motorcyclist is not easy . . . the strain, the worry – but a wife should be a help and not a hinderance. Barry's family means everything to him and he's the first to admit that his wife Junie has been a constant inspiration.

I F you think that the life of the professional motor cycle racer is hectic, being married to one is no less so. A wife can be a help or a hindrance to a single-minded rider who wants to be at the top of his profession all the time. Barry seems quite satisfied, though, and has even put it on the record, publicly!

It goes without saying that one has to support, help, encourage, advise and commiserate. The trick is to know when to do what. But after 17 years I know pretty well how Barry thinks and reacts under any given set of circumstances and the good times far outnumber the bad.

Racing has brought us so much – a nice home, lots of travel, so many friends. But it hasn't just been a means to an end. It has been a way of life and, as far as Barry is concerned, the way of life. Now he is riding less, he can pick and choose what he wants to do, and when. But even so, looking at his schedule

on the continent this year, I'm only amazed that he used to do this *and* the British League as well.

I am glad that he came to the decision to retire from regular British speedway himself. I wouldn't have wanted to put pressure on him to give up before he was ready. All the same, in some ways it has been a relief to me.

The last couple of years (1971 and 1972) were very trying. Barry had so much bad luck with his bikes, and spent so much time worrying about those problems, that his own appetite for racing was almost bound to suffer. And when he brought those worries home, inevitably the strain and pressure built up.

Barry recognised this himself. He said the last thing he wanted was to let his problems affect me or the boys. And I think this may have had some influence on his decision. For the last year or two, he had been toying with the idea of cutting down on his

57

commitments. What kept him going as much as anything was the thought that he was still good enough to win the World Final.

After 1971 had been such a bad year – the biggest disappointment was getting knocked out of the championships at the British/Nordic Final in Glasgow – he more or less decided that '72 was to be the 'now or never year'.

I couldn't believe it when he was knocked out at Glasgow. After all, he had been in the Final for 17 years on the trot and even though his bikes were playing up, nobody thought he would go out at this stage. When he rang up that evening and I asked how he'd got on, he just said: 'I'm out.' It was incredible.

After missing out there, Barry had a good think about his future and in the next few months you could tell that he was building up to a really big effort in the next championships. Virtually everything he did and said in connection with speedway had this message running through it: '1972 is going to be THE year.'

There had been big years before. After all, he'd won the championship four times and been near on several other occasions. Being second, though, didn't mean anything to him any more. He wanted one more win, which would put him level with Ove (Fundin) and more than that, would show that he could still do it.

Everybody wants to go out at the top and, especially after Glasgow, there were some people who reckoned Barry had gone over the top. He was still capable of beating virtually anybody, anywhere, but after all that he'd done, any suggestion of a slip was enough for the critics.

But he has always been a good judge of his own capabilities. And because he was as fit as ever, and as keen – if not more so – than ever, of course he had a tremendous chance at Wembley this time.

Despite all those pre-season hopes, there were lots of problems during the first few months. The bike worries of the previous year seemed to be multiplied this time. There were ups and downs, a fortnight's break away from it all, a return with renewed enthusiasm, then more disappointments, injuries; it went on and on.

But as the Final drew nearer, the confidence came dashing back. Barry was getting chirpier all the time. It wasn't just foolish confidence, either; he doesn't react that way. Simply, he was growing in his belief that the title was there for the taking because he was in shape, he had a bike that was just right for the Final, and in every way the whole campaign was falling into place.

When he went to Wembley for the World Final there is no doubt he was going to win it. And if anybody doubted it beforehand, his win over Ivan (Mauger) in his first race was the best possible start he could have had.

It didn't work out, of course. He had that spill in his second ride. At the time I didn't think too much of it. After all, Barry had taken tumbles before.

After all this time, I'm not the sort to get hysterical and I don't believe in rushing off to see what has happened, getting in everybody's way and confusing the whole issue. Quite simply, I have this faith in Barry's ability to look after himself, and if he is hurt, faith in people's ability to administer the appropriate medical treatment.

Anyway, Barry was down, but surely he would be up in a minute. He always got up. Except this time he didn't. This time he was lifted on a stretcher and carried off.

I was sitting up in the stands with Ronnie Moore and eventually he said: 'I'm going down to see what's happened – are you coming?'

'Oh no – he's probably only winded,' I replied, still quite confident. I expected him to be out for the rerun of his race at any moment.

But a few minutes later Ronnie came back and waved to me to come down. He told me that Barry had a nasty injury to his left hand and that we had to go to hospital.

We really started to be worried when the hospital people didn't quite know what was the best thing to do. They were equipped for all sorts of casualties, but with over-stating the importance of one person over another, Barry's was not a simple case.

It would have been the same if he had been a musician or anything like that: clearly only the opinion of a highly-qualified specialist would do. But there was nobody at the hospital who could give that sort of opinion and nobody contactable either, or so it seemed.

Eventually I managed to contact our old friend Dr. Carlo Biagi in Scotland, and had him discuss the situation with the doctors at the Middlesex hospital Eventually, it was decided that Barry would have to lose his left index finger. It wasn't a pleasant thought, but as always with speedway injuries you think that there are worse accidents which could befall you.

The pandemonium on that Saturday night won't easily be forgotten. But how would it have been if Barry had received head injuries instead of a damanged hand?

All the to-ing and fro-ing didn't have such serious consequences, as it turned out. But all riders are more worried about their heads than anything and we have known riders, friends, who have died simply because expert knowledge wasn't immediately available after a track crash.

I firmly believe that each track should have better medical facilities than exist at most places. And there should be a list of specialists in different forms of treatment and experts on various injuries . . . top men who could perhaps be paid a retainer so that they were available on call if and when a speedway rider was sufficiently badly hurt to need their attention in a hurry.

There isn't a single aspect of speedway more important than safety. We all know the hazards. If one stopped to think about them too much, too often, it wouldn't be long before you end up as a nervous wreck. Just because neither riders, nor wives, like to dwell upon this aspect of racing, it is futile to say: 'It couldn't happen to me.'

Accidents do occur. Almost without exception the riders realise that the sport is as dangerous as they make it. Everybody wants to see tomorrow so ridiculous conduct on the track rarely occurs, and when it does it is not tolerated. But things can go wrong.

Riders probably think about the injury aspect less than wives. For us it is always present in the back of the mind. When your man is racing, the first thought, always, is: is he all right? Whether he has scored 15 points or half-a-dozen isn't the most important thing.

All the same, success and the pursuit of success has always been of vital importance to Barry. From a very early stage he decided that he wanted to be the top rider and he has worked hard to be among the world's best for longer than almost any other rider.

Barry, the 'raver', with his wife June at a speedway social evening.

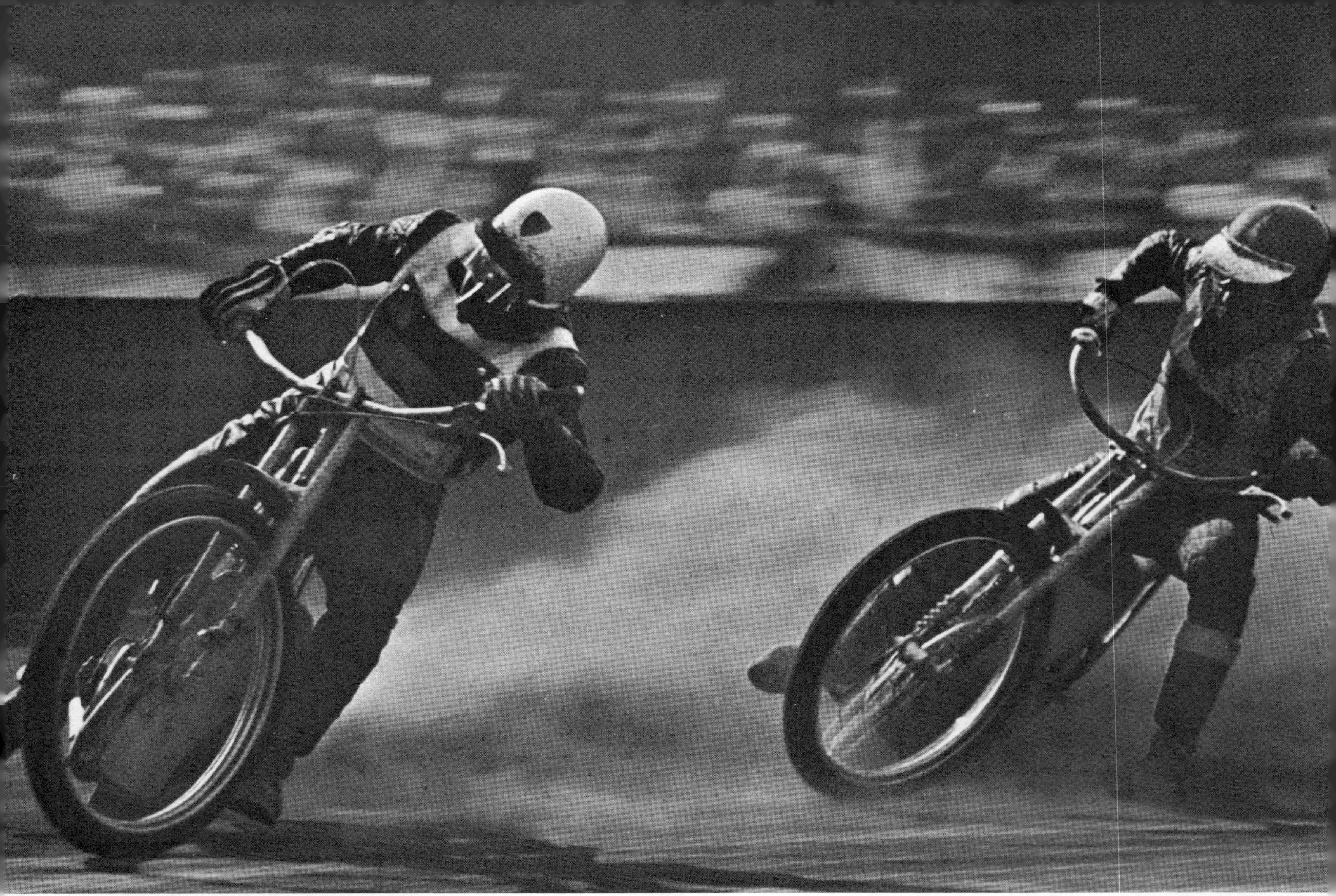

Hans Jurgen Fritz leads Manfred

The Briggs family in action . . . (left to right) Tony, Gary and Barry.

Naturally enough, one shares his triumphs and disappointments equally. When the good times come along, that's fine. But it can be hard work, trying to encourage or commiserate when times are difficult. It isn't always too easy to appreciate and understand the temperament of somebody who can go through so many varying moods.

When a weekend trip is coming up, and the arrangements are not falling absolutely into place, all hell is let loose. If you have been connected with racing, this is quite common – but it is difficult for somebody on the outside to comprehend.

For example, when Barry comes back from a European trip, he always puts away his international licence in the same place. But when the time for departure on the next trip comes up, he can never find it. Invariably we have a few words and a frantic search.

Inevitably I suppose we tend to move towards people who have, or have had, some speedway connection or at least a sporting connection – because they know how it is and don't consider such behaviour at all remarkable!

When an overseas jaunt, or a big championship meeting here, or anything of that sort, is coming up, the atmosphere in and around the house changes. Barry, inevitably, is getting himself built up and obviously some of this rubs off on me and on Gary and Tony as well. Yet in spite of all this, I wouldn't trade any of it. Barry is doing what he does best and loves most.

And if speedway has brought its share of worries and problems, the good times are the ones you remember. I have made so many friends in the sport. Most of the wives are very nice and we all understand one another well enough.

I have a few particular friends, people like Raye Mauger – whom we knew when he first came over in 1957 – Cynthia Boocock and, of course, Ronnie's wife Jill. But a lot of the old ones are no longer connected with speedway.

At Belle Vue for the British Riders' Final last October, I was able to watch the meeting without worrying – because Barry wasn't able to ride – but I felt a bit of an outsider.

It makes me a little sad, too, when I notice some of the attitudes a few riders' wives have these days. It seems different from a few years ago. Now they will think nothing of shouting for another member of their team against Barry even though we're supposed to be friends! If it's their own husband they are shouting for I don't mind and wouldn't expect anything else.

There is bound to be a little rivalry and sometimes jealousy between some of the wives but in the end we're all prejudiced towards the old man and maybe that doesn't make for being the best and most objective judge of a situation!

It annoys me when people score off somebody else – and while the wives can scratch their eyes out if they want to, I don't like riders who have knocked Barry.

He has helped and befriended so many of them, but in recent years there were always those who would accept his friendship and then do the dirty on him. Of all the disappointments he has had, none hurt more than at the British/Nordic championship meeting at West Ham in 1968.

Barry was knocked out, which was bad enough, but he was promised some help by people he helped in the past – and didn't get any. There were too many people prepared to laugh at his misfortune and to cap it all he had some equipment and a couple of new wheels piched after the meeting.

I have never known him so disillusioned.

He's much less hard than people imagine and you cannot always believe what people say. When he started at Wimbledon he was supposed to be a real tearaway but in fact he was so shy it was untrue. When I first knew him, it was three months before he actually stepped over the front step into my parents' house. He used to knock timidly at the door, ask if I was in, and would prefer to wait outside. When we finally did persuade him that he wasn't

A tremendous welcome awaited Barry Briggs and Ivan Mauger when they arrived at Los Angeles International Airport a few years back. Left to right: Steve Bass, June Briggs, Barry Briggs, Cheryl Funk, Ivan Mauger, Raye Mauger.

Briggo (arrowed) watches the 1971 European Final at Wembley. Barry was eliminated from the World Championship in the previous round at Glasgow.

going to be eaten, it was another three months before he could bring himself to accept the offer of a cup of tea.

Obviously he is rather more out-going now and travelling and racing all round the world, we meet all sorts of people. Nothing bothers him now but he is still completely unassuming and I've never known him put on any airs and graces.

Because he is so genuine, he gets on best with people who are basically straight and nice. Some of our most treasured friendships are with people whose names mean absolutely nothing to the speed-way public, but who have helped and encouraged Barry so much down the years. The ends to which people will put themselves out sometimes is un-believable, humbling really.

And those are the sort of people who enjoy Barry's success just as much as he does himself.

Despite being a top star, mixing with important people, and – thanks to racing – enjoying a good standard of living, Barry genuinely hasn't changed that much.

Since settling down in Southampton and with Gary and Tony growing up, we have become a family instead of just a partnership and that's made it all the better. Although he is always rushing off here and there and everywhere, Barry still spends more time with the boys than most parents and they both think the world of him.

The next problem, I suppose, will be deciding whether they want to start racing. Both are mad keen on motor cycles but it's just fun and enjoyment for them at the moment.

I'm not too sure how I'll react if they do want to race professionally. What's more, I don't want to think about it for a year or two!

63

BRIGGO in the U.S.A.

TOP LEFT: Barry Briggs, riding on the indoor circuit in Jacksonville. BOTTOM LEFT: A concerned Briggo stands over one of his his best mates, Keith Mashburn . . . Barry had just knocked him off! TOP RIGHT: The A.M.A. American Championships — Barry is shown passing the top two American riders (denoted by the numbers of their bikes) Mert Lawill (1) and Dick 'Buggsy' Mann (2). There is nothing they can do as Briggo comes round the outside at the Santa Fe track in Chicago. BOTTOM RIGHT: Barry Briggs, on a Yamaha, at the Astrodome in Houston, Texas.

ABOVE: Pawel Waloszek of Poland — a fine action shot. BELOW: Ole Olsen of Denmark, covered in shale after a race in which he has uncharacteristically been behind.

ABOVE: Ivan Mauger and Swedish star Bengt Jansson between races. BELOW: Nigel Boocock and Anders Michanek contest the lead during an international at Belle Vue.

'The greatest double-jointed World Champion of all time.' Ove Fundin is the rider. Note the left leg.

ABOVE: Igor Plechanov, the victor at a meeting in Czechoslovakia, with Barry Briggs second and Boris Samarodov third. Notice the young crowd. The Russians got a bad reception at this event, held shortly after the Soviet invasion of Czechoslovakia, which embarrassed Barry. 'The Russkies are 100 per cent lads,' he says, 'and I hate to see politics creeping into sport'. BELOW: Briggs on the outside, Nigel Boocock inside, but who's in the middle with the Russian-type handlebars? It's Ole Olsen, back in 1966. RIGHT: Those famous 'Briggo wheelies' – one in Germany and the other at the 1957 Daily Mirror Cavalcade of Sport at the White City.

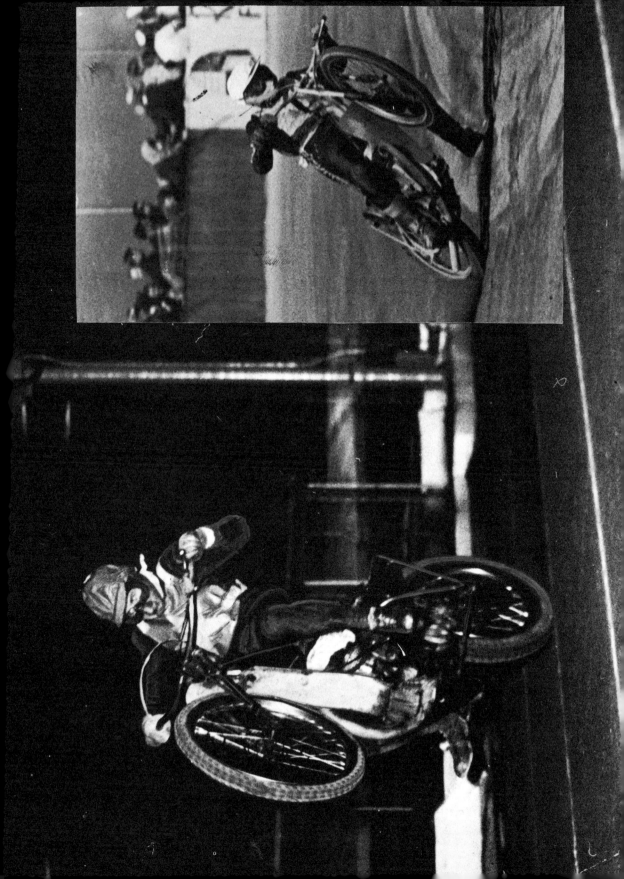

Ole Olsen . . . World Champion in 1971 and a brilliant rider.

ABOVE: Autograph hunting at the 'Glen Campbell Pro-Am' golf meeting in California. Tony and Gary Briggs corner Glen Campbell and (BELOW) Tony gets Andy Williams to sign on. TOP RIGHT: Briggo fueling Ivan Mauger - is this the secret of Ivan's success? BOTTOM RIGHT: Briggo's first trophy after his World Final crash at Wembley won at Napier in New Zealand.

On the road

IT was mid-way through November 1972 when Briggo first told me of his decision to quit regular British League racing. He perched himself on the edge of a desk in my London office and said simply: 'I've had a great run and I don't think I have to prove myself to anyone anymore. I reckon the time is ripe to call it a day, so I suppose we had better start letting people know.'

He said it calmly and matter-of-factly, and it was obvious he'd given the decision a great deal of thought. Mind you, it wasn't entirely unexpected – although he hadn't said anything, I knew that retirement had been at the back of his mind for quite some time.

Over the next few days, I formulated plans to make Barry's decision known to the public at large. We met and talked a couple of times, and discussed how we should go about things. I was determined that his illustrious career should end with a bang and not a whimper, and the more I thought about it, the clearer it became that we should try to make the announcement via television and not the press – in that way we were sure to reach a mass audience.

And that's exactly what happened. One Saturday afternoon Barry sat down opposite TV interviewer Dickie Davies on 'World of Sport' – and within minutes, countless millions of avid sports fans were aware that British League racing was to lose its most colourful and spectacular star.

Setting up that TV appearance was also my swansong in speedway. After a five-year association with Briggo in a managerial and publicity capacity – plus a short spell handling press for Ray Wilson and three years on the administrative staff of the now-defunct Crayford track – I found that I had finally cut all my ties with the sport.

In some ways I'm sorry because I always enjoy good racing. I like the social side of things, too – speedway riders are a special breed and there's a

Typical action at a grass-track meeting in West Germany. Manfred Poschenreider is nearest the camera.

with Briggo

fundamental honesty and integrity about them that is all too rare in today's complex world.

But since the start of the seventies, I have become increasingly aware that the sport is riddled with major faults. The sad state of refereeing, a tangled rule book that largely seems to be ignored, unacceptable schemes like rider allocation and guest riders, an international selection code that allows a Scotsman to ride for England . . . these are just a few of the things that have soured my attitude towards speedway. But for all that, I have happy memories of the game – and the happiest stem from the many occasions I have travelled the continent with this remarkable man Briggs.

There's nothing quite like life on the road for getting a deep and thorough insight into a man's personality, and after jaunts through West Germany, Czechoslovakia, Belgium, France and Scandanavia – acting as manager, publicist, car navigator, male nurse, interpreter, spare parts salesman, occasional mechanic (no kidding – I really can tell a clutch plate from an exhaust pipe and general troubleshooter, I reckon I know this Briggo character pretty well.

First off, you get to learn that he's a perfectionist – a complete professional who is totally dedicated to his chosen job. He accepts that just so long as an audience pay to watch him, he's in show business and therefore has a duty to the public.

He fully understands the meaning of the show business term, too . . . talk a deal with him and you soon see that he has a better-than-good business head on his shoulders. And as for the show – well, has there ever been a more exciting, all-action, value-for-money rider in the game? It's true Briggo has made a lot of money from racing; it's equally true that he has taken no more from the sport than he has justly earned, and earned the hard way!

The man has a pretty wild sense of humour. Sure he's moody at times; especially so immediately prior to the start of a race meeting when he understandably has a lot of things on his mind. But basically,

Nobody knows better than KEITH GOODWIN what it is like to travel across Europe as part of the Briggs' entourage... here he recalls some of the humorous anecdotes.

he's a pretty happy fellow and you'd have to go a long way to find a better travelling companion.

I first went on the road with him back in 1968 – a trip to Czechoslovakia for business meetings at the ESO factory just outside Prague, followed by a couple of days in West Germany where Barry was trying his hand at ice-racing for the first time. The air trip over was fine, but we hit our first snag when we hopped in a car at Prague airport.

You see, Barry doesn't smoke, and I do. He kept quiet for a couple of miles, then started to make snide remarks about filthy, dirty habits. I was a bit of a chain smoker at the time, and every time I lit up, he groaned and huddled tighter into his corner of the back seat. Finally he couldn't stand it anymore and with much muttering and blaspheming, wound down all the windows.

A simple solution? Not with an outside temperature around 10 below zero and banks of snow on either side of the road. Eventually we settled on a compromise – I wouldn't smoke just so long as he kept his hairy mits off the window handles!

I got my initial taste of his sense of humour that first might in Prague. We ambled around the city for a while, then found a nice little restaurant where – among other things – they served a particularly potent brand of red wine that tasted like a combination of San Izal and Airwick. Being a non-drinker, Briggo wouldn't get near the stuff; on the other hand, being something of an idiot, I managed to down a couple of bottles.

I don't recall the journey back to our motel, but I do remember dropping on my knees and praying for sleep before climbing into bed. The wardrobe was just about to start its third tour of the room, and I was quietly contemplating a rapid dash to the bathroom, when the 'phone rang. It just had to be Briggo. It was.

'Quick,' he yelled down the'phone, doing a pretty fair imitation of a lion at feeding time. 'Get to the window – there's a great striptease going on.'

Now even with 50 little men inside my head, banging bloody great hammers on bloody great anvils, I'm not averse to the idea of watching a dolly bird get 'em off. So I lurched out of bed, tripped over cases, banged my shins on a table but finally made it to the window – in time to watch a hairy great Czech gent silhouetted as he dropped his pants in the lighted window of the room opposite mine.

Briggo laughed like a drain the next morning and despite my pale face and an appearance closely resembling death, slapped me continually on the back and insisted I go with him to some sort of export agency to sort out some paper work. At the agency, he was 100 per cent efficiency – checking forms, signing papers galore and generally wheeling and dealing in a very impressive manner.

So efficient, in fact, that there was precious little for me to do. So I wandered off in search of black coffee and was on my second cup in a quiet, tatty little cafe down the road when a couple of jack-booted policemen walked ominously towards me.

Now these weren't your actual 'Please can you tell me the time' type coppers . . . this twosome carried shoulder-arms and re-volvers and looked more like fugitives from a James Bond film. 'Papers,' they demanded. I didn't happen to have my passport with me so I did the only thing possible: offered dogeared copies of the 'Daily Mirror' and 'Daily Express'. Their faces turned all shades of purple, and although I couldn't understand a word they said. I somehow knew they weren't exactly amused.

Enter Briggo . . . striding through the door and sporting a wide grin like a cat that's just got the cream. Over the next few minutes, I learned another thing about Barry – he's an incredible diplomat. Now you have to understand that Barry doesn't speak more than a word or two of Czech (his English isn't too hot, either, but that's another story). Yet within minutes, he'd got his arms around the shoulders of the two giant cops and they're all laughing insanely and slapping each other on the back like they'd known each other all their lives.

It's impossible, I tell you, but it happened. Before we eventually got out of the place, he'd even got Swindon Speedway badges pinned to the lapels of their coats and I fully expected to see tickets for the next Swindon dinner/dance pulled from his pockets. I've seen him pull this sort of caper so many times, but I still don't know how he gets away with it.

I suppose it's a mixture of genuine charm, an infectious grin and a very persuasive personality. In any event, I'm convinced that Barry can talk his way out of anything, and language barriers will never be any sort of problem to him.

Before we leave Prague, let me tell you a little about the ESO factory. It's a grey, cold building – lifeless from the outside but a veritable hive of bustle and activity inside. Sixty per cent of the workers who assemble the speedway machines are women; and at least fifty per cent of the women are built like brick outhouses! One of them, a delicate little creature who tips the scales around twenty stone, picked up a complete bike and lifted it three feet on to a table.

But what marvellous people. They are kind, considerate and thoughtful to a fault. In fact, I've found that the Czech people are among the nicest I've ever met. They appear to have very little, yet they seldom complain.

Whenever Briggo goes to the factory, he takes along three or four cases of Coca Cola to hand around – which is the equivalent there of being handed a bottle of champagne here. The factory people are Briggo fans to a man (or 'woman') and he knows them all . . . from the guy who sweeps the floor up to the Managing Director. He's liked *and* respected (which is important because there is a difference) and it's easy to comprehend why Barry has such a rewarding relationship with the ESO organisation.

One of the prime reasons for our visit to the

74

Briggo's first ever
long-track meeting
at Kiel in Germany.
Notice the big helmet –
Barry used to find that it
would blow off when
travelling at over
100 m.p.h.

Barry Briggs (70) riding a Yamaha at Houston. Ivan Mauger is number 60.

factory on that occasion was to pick up an ice bike. Barry tried it out briefly on a frozen pond a few yards from the factory before we set off on the long drive to Inzell, a West German winter resort close to the Austrian border. Apart from grass track specialist Don Godden, who was holidaying nearby and came along to lend a mechanical hand, I reckon I'm the only Englishman ever to have seen Barry ride the ice in a full-scale competitive meeting – and it's an experience I won't forget.

In recent years, a handful of English riders have tried their hands at ice-racing with varying degrees of success. None have attained anything like world championship status – but had he given the sport his undivided attention, I'm convinced Barry could have been the world's first non-European champion.

This was the first time Barry had been on ice, remember, come to think of it, it was also the first time he'd ever seen the sport, let alone take part. Yet in the face of world class opposition, he took fourth place behind the eventual winner, Sweden's Bernt Hornfeldt. A third place in his first outing, then a good second – and Barry had got the hang of things.

In his next three rides, he demolished the opposition to collect nine points. I just wish some British fans had been there to see Briggo proving that

ice-racing need not necessarily be the exclusive domain of the Russians and Swedes.

Watching ice-racing for the first time is quite an eye-opener. The Inzell meeting was an open air affair on a 400-metre track normally used for speed skating. There's no conventional safety fence – just a four-foot thick wall of solid ice. This does the trick in no uncertain manner. Racing took place in conditions not far removed from freezing point, so it wasn't surprising to see machanics boiling the oil over primus stoves before they started preparing the machines for racing. The motor gets quite a going over with a blow lamp during the warming up period and every rider keeps a stock of heavy blankets to pile on his machine to preserve some sort of warmth between races.

Because of the total traction with the ice surface when cornering – thanks to heavily-spiked front and rear wheels – riders are able to lay their machines at seemingly impossible angles. Old-fashioned leg trailing is imperative (those that attempt the contemporary foot-forward style usually wind up with a mouthful of gums after a nodding acquaintance with the solid ice 'safety' fence) and in many cases riders take a phenomenal amount of weight and strain on their left forearm, which slides along the ice when cornering.

For protection, old car tyres are cut up and strapped along the right forearm and elbow and over the left knee-cap. Believe me, it's quite a performance preparing for ice-racing . . and when you realise that all this has to be done in brass-monkey conditions, it's not exactly a picnic.

Still, Briggo didn't take long to get into the routine. With the aid of Don Godden and West German speedway and long-track star Manfred Poschenreider, he made meticulous preparations for the meeting because he was determined to do well. And, as I've already said, he did just that. Ice-racing is both frightening and spectacular – a severe test for iron nerves, split-second timing and control. I thought it was the most exciting form of motor cycle racing I'd ever seen – until they brought on the sidecar merchants!

Sidecars on ice? Too right – and those chairs really move. It's not so bad at first, when the ice surface is pretty smooth. But after half a dozen races, the ice really cuts up rough and the passengers in the sidecars get buffeted around like nobody's business. After watching one hectic sidecar event, Briggo walked away muttering: 'They've got to be mad.' Thus spoke a man who has broken virtually every bone in his body!

It was during those early continental trips with Barry that I learned about his eating habits. Basically, he likes things plain and simple . . . and he worships the fried potato in the same way as other people worship God. To every half pound of grilled steak, he needs around a pound of chips. If the Government ever decided to ban potatoes (don't laugh, politicians have already done dafter things!) I think Barry would fade away and die. When we used to stop at a motorway cafe, I thought at first Barry's love of plain food was due solely to the fact that he didn't know enough German and could only handle orders for steak, pork chops and his beloved oxtail soup.

I used to try to press more exotic dishes on him. If I explained that the dish came with chips, he showed a mild interest for a moment of two. But after a couple of minutes of deep, concentrated thought, he'd smile benignly at me, growl a few words of strangled German at a passing waiter and wind up with a massive steak – and chips.

The promoter of a meeting in Straubing once asked us to stay overnight at his home and the following morning presented us with a continental-style breakfast that had Briggo growling un-complimentary obscentities almost before he'd sat down at the table. Faced with an under-boiled egg, assorted pieces of cheese, thick black bread, a variety of jams and a complete absence of butter, Barry blanched visibly and pleadingly raised his eyes upwards.

I am convinced somebody up there must like him because within minutes, our host seemed to have got the message and was offering scrambled eggs and bacon.

On another occasion we spent a solid hour scouring Ostend – at three o'clock in the morning – for Barry's bloody chips. We'd travelled around 400 miles non-stop and we were both very tired, hungry and thirsty. There were plenty of little cafes selling hot-dogs, hamburgers, even sandwiches. But no – Briggo had to have chips, from one of the little curbside stalls.

'Best chips in the world,' he kept telling me. Could be – but at three o'clock in the morning, I'd have happily settled for a sawdust sand-wich instead of driving aimlessly around Ostend. Eventually, we found a little old man who was just about to shut up shop. Barry bought every chip in sight, then sat down on the curb with a contented sigh and tucked in like there was no tomorrow.

There's a bit of a postscript story to that night . . . something I've never let Briggo forget. An hour after the Great Chip Search, we boarded the Ostend ferry. Since I was still hungry, he urged me to eat one of the foul-smelling sausages in captivity in one of the snackbars. That was my first mistake.

My second was to take a sleeping berth somewhere deep in the bowels of the boat – once again on Briggo's advice. For a start, I couldn't get to sleep thanks to Barry's snoring – God, how he snores! And then, once out of the harbour, the ship started to roll . . . I mean R.O.L.L. I don't think I've ever felt so ill in my life.

Briggo snored happily through it all while I flung every insult in the book at Neptune and all his cronies behind a toilet door. At Dover Customs, Briggo had a groaning, gibbering invalid on his hands; but at least my pale face and heaving

A fine action shot of Ove Fundin riding at Kempton, West Germany

stomach convinced the custom official that he should clear us pretty quickly and Briggo – grinning broadly and occasionally asking if I fancied a bacon-and-egg breakfast – drove me back to London. You know, I haven't been on a boat since.

It's well-known that as well as being a non-smoker, Barry is also a non-drinker. But just once during our friendship have I known him take a drink. Not a big one, mind . . . just a sip, really, but I believe he enjoyed it. It happened in France in 1969, and when I say that Barry is a creature of impulse, this little story is abundant proof of that claim.

It was July – a hot, consistently sunny July in Cavaliere, in the South of France, where I was on holiday with my wife Pat. Just before I left England, Barry had been involved in an alarming crash and broken his right arm and wrist. We sent him a holiday card, showing the hotel and surrounding beaches and, being something of a dab hand at original phrases, wrote on it: 'Wish you were here.'

A couple of days later, I was lying on the beach near the terrace when a stone hit me on the head. Not a big one, but enough to make me yelp. A minute went by – then a slightly bigger stone clouts

me on the ankle. Still I refused to move or open my eyes – what the hell, I'm on holiday. Then half a housebrick plops on to my bare navel. Swearing vengeance on the nearest unattended child with a sickly, innocent smile on his face, I leapt up – and there, sitting on the wall, trousers rolled up to the knees, right arm encased in plaster and left arm round the waist of a delicious blond known as Mrs Briggs is Barry.

'You're getting fat,' he announces, dispensing with the customary greetings. There really isn't an answer to that sort of opening. 'Can't race with this,' he went on, indicating the plastered arm, 'so I thought I'd come and annoy you.' Just like that – a creature of impulse.

After a bit of haggling, we managed to fix Barry and June up with a room, and within a couple of days, he'd become quite a focal point of interest among the hotel guests. Nothing to do with his film star good looks and boyish charm but purely on account of his plastered arm. You see, nothing so trivial as a broken wing was going to keep Briggo out of the water. Every morning and afternoon, regular as clockwork, he used to go for a swim.

He'd walk out until the water reached his neck,

then launch himself like a torpedo. Everything would be under water – head, neck, shoulders; everything, that is, except his plastered right arm, which he had to keep dry. It used to stick straight up like a periscope and people used to gather on the seashore to watch. They'd never seen anything like it before and I doubt if they ever will again.

Most of the people who go to Cavaliere in July are 'regulars' so Pat and I know them pretty well. Naturally enough, they asked questions about the underwater swimmer with the built-in periscope. I managed to get across that he was a world champion but they were all completely in the dark about speedway. Eventually I handed round a copy of *Speedway Star* – an edition which happened to include a lot of good action shots and some terrifying pile-up pictures.

Our friends studied the pictures, eyed Barry's broken arm, and concluded that there must be easier ways of earning a living. Seriously, though,

Barry made a lot of friends and as an ambassador for sport in general and speedway in particular, he came through with flying colours.

We spent a lot of time playing a curious French game called Boule. Broadly speaking, it's akin to bowls – except that you use heavy metal balls instead of wooden ones and play on rough ground instead of hallowed turf. Briggo got pretty good at the game – but not nearly as good as Bert Croucher, the former Wembley and Southampton speedway star who is Briggo's next-door neighbour.

Barry and June were so impressed with Cavaliere that they telephoned 'Cocky' and asked him down for a few days. We had quite a little speedway fraternity going. Towards the end of our vacation, the hotel staged a Boule tournament; we'd left by the time the final was staged, but Bert stayed on and won the trophy!

Now, about that drink I was telling you about.

Pictured at the Ernie Roccio Memorial Meeting in California are Cindy Roccio, Sonny Nutter, Pete Palmer and Jimmy Lennon (announcer).

One evening we walked into the hotel restaurant for dinner, and I headed for our usual table. At first I thought that another party had got in first because there on the table was a magnum of champagne. I started to look around for another table, but Barry and June sat down, and motioned for Pat and I to do likewise.

Still in the dark, I reached for a card on the bottle and read: 'Happy Birthday from June & Barry.' You know, I'd forgotten my own birthday. But, typical of the thoughtfulness of this man Briggs, he'd remembered. So I popped the cork and poured four glasses. Barry was dubious at first. 'It's only bubbly water,' I insisted. Still he was undecided. Then he looked around at the three expectant faces goading him on, raised his glass and said 'Happy Birthday Keek.'

'Keek,' I should explain, is one of the many strange ways Barry has of saying my name. He's also prone to address me as 'Hairy' and at one particular long track meeting in Germany in the late sixties,

he took it into his head to tell everybody that I was The Beatles manager, which caused no end of confusion because a lot of people believed him. The autograph hunters and ticket sneakers didn't pose too many problems, but it got a bit embarrassing when a couple of nicely-formed teenaged girls announced they would do *anything* if I would take them back to England to meet Ringo!

I was asked for a few anecdotes about life on the road with Briggo and I could go on for hours recalling hilarious episodes in half a dozen countries. But there simply isn't either the time or the space to tell everything in one go, so I've deliberately chosen lighthearted moments to recapture.

Perhaps we can look at other aspects of the Briggo personality another day. He really is a complex character, and there's a serious side to him that is deserving of detailed examination.

But that's another story – and, hopefully, the subject for another book about one of the nicest guys ever to get involved in the world of sport.

Miroslav Verner of Czechoslovakia

Barry with the glamorous Cheryl Funk in America

ROUND THE WORLD

Terry Betts of Great Britain leads Jan Simensen (Sweden) and Viktor Kalmykov (Russia) during the 1972 World Team Cup Final at Olching.

Barry Briggs (inside) leads Doug Davies of South Africa during a test match in South Africa. Davies' left foot takes a battering from Briggo's bike.

A pre-meeting parade at Christchurch in New Zealand with Ronnie Moore, Ivan Mauger and Barry Briggs on the leading car.

Barry Briggs leads Josef Kamper during a visit to Austria some years ago.

TOP LEFT: It always pays to make the start at a grass track meeting in West Germany . . . as the unfortunate number 59 finds out. BELOW LEFT: You've heard about over-watering tracks, but this is ridiculous! ABOVE: Picture of the year? A German rider learns that everything that goes up, must come down — but he remembers to keep an eye on his machine. BELOW: No prizes for guessing this duo.

GUESS WHO?

Brigg

LEFT: Briggo in America with Bruce Brown (centre), who made the film 'On Any Sunday' and Malcolm Smith, the star of the film. BELOW: Barry with his great mate, Chelsea footballer David Webb. RIGHT: Top film star Steve McQueen and Briggo after a racing session in the States.

and friends

TOP: Barry Briggs' first and only ice-racing event at Inzell. Barry is shown leading the eventual winner, Bernt Hornfeldt.

LEFT: Briggo's first ride on a 650cc, 130mph, Yamaha at the half-mile San Jose track in California. RIGHT: The story of Barry's life . . . the end of a day's racing at Pardubice in Czechoslovakia after bike trouble. Dietev Dauderev, Briggo's mechanic that day, retrieves the machine.

JOHN LOUIS
of Ipswich

'POPE JOHN'

An assessment of Tiger Louis by BARRY BRIGGS

ONE of the most important and exciting newcomers on the racing scene in recent times is John Louis, the Ipswich boy who burst into prominence last year. John – 'The Pope' as I call him – must be England's best world championship prospect if he gets the breaks. You need a bit of luck along the way. But you also need a load of other credentials, and this bloke has them.

He has the right attitude, and that is very important. He wants to learn all the time, and he doesn't need telling twice. John gives all his time to racing and he doesn't have any hang-ups about different tracks, difficult conditions or anything like that. He used to be a good moto-cross rider and after doing well on that, you don't bother to complain if a speedway circuit happens to be a bit choppy!

Why 'The Pope' you might wonder? It's back to one of his early meetings in Italy. If you think John's fans at Ipswich give him enthusiastic support, you should see those Italians... they make a real carnival out of an occassion like the visit of a handful of racers from England.

Anyway, he's a big hero at Montagnana and there were loads of placards praising John, including one which bore the legend: 'John Louis for King'. I suggested that Pope would be a more fitting office and it's stuck ... much to John's embarrassment. He doesn't ruffle easily, though, which must be one of the reasons for his phenomenal rate of progress. Two

or three years back nobody had even heard of him. Then he took the Second Division by storm, and after a dodgy start, did much the same in the First Division last year.

There is always some new sensation coming along. One becomes aware of these fellows and notice who is going good. But before last year just about all I knew of him was when he delivered a moto-cross bike to West Ham for me, one day back in 1970. At that time John was still working for Dave Bickers in Ipswich and naturally it was interesting to compare a few notes: Dave imports the Jawa scramble bikes just as I have the concession for speedway motorcycles.

Although Bickers never took to speedway – which was a pity because he is another of those natural motor cyclists and a great character, too – Louis must have picked up something from him. Getting better, meeting class opposition, coming to terms with the new demands which come along as you improve – it can be a difficult business but Louis probably couldn't have a better mentor than Dave.

At the same time, though, what he's achieved he has done because he has this ability. However much

The 1972 Wills Internationale at Wimbledon . . . Ivan Mauger leads John Louis, Trevor Hedge and Garry Middleton.

somebody helps you, points you in the right direction, it's down to you in the end. And when Louis started scoring well and consistently, I wasn't the only one to sit up and take notice. Everybody flies at some time but the real test is whether the rider can sustain it. Once Louis got the taste of winning he decided he liked the sensation so much that he wasn't going to let go.

Because he stayed in the Second Division in 1971, I didn't see much of him, although in the Olympique handicap meeting at Wolverhampton he shaped well. Nothing over brilliant but clearly he was one to watch. He did very well in another open meeting at Reading and Martin Ashby was telling me just how impressive John looked. Apparently he had done really well there in scratch conditions and against a lot of the good boys.

Ipswich got their place in the First Division after West Ham pulled out and John was good and ready. There were a lot of people who didn't think he would fare too well. They said the same about Ivan Mauger when the Provincial League finished and we all went in together in 1965. The difference with Ivan was that after two years of beating every-body in the Provincial League, his opportunity to prove himself against the former National League blokes was spoiled by injury. He smashed himself up pretty good and despite a brave effort in the World Championships, it was something of a wasted first year for him.

John didn't have any such misfortune. He straight away got stuck into all the top merchants and for the first few weeks it was tough. He had bike problems, too. He was winning some but losing as many and I feel that it was when he started doing well on the continent that his home form also started to come good.

I was due to ride a Saturday night meeting at Swindon and then go to Montagnana the following day. The only thing to do was to fly out and I telephoned John, who was also in the same meeting, to see if he could take my bike down there. He seemed quite happy to do that, especially as I said I'd reimburse him for any extra costs incurred. He'd been there for an earlier meeting, when there were not so many of the top names there – I missed it and Ivan was somewhere else – and had done so well that they fell over themselves to get him back.

This was going to be a much tougher test but he passed with flying colours and won the meeting. He beat Garry Middleton in the run-off for first place. I'd had some trouble – this was in the spell of spring madness which almost caused me to give it away – but in spite of my own problems I couldn't help being impressed with the Ipswich boy. I found that he had a terrific temperament; you could joke with him and he wasn't at all wound up.

It was a bad day for me. The bike blew up in practice, and first I borrowed a standard speedway bike, and then another machine from Sture Lindblom, the Swede. The back fell out of the tank on that! But seeing Louis cope with everything was a real reward. I tipped him off on a couple of details of technique, and gave him a bit of advice before he met Middleton. He paid so much attention and then went and did just as I had suggested better than I would have hoped to do it myself.

The next time I saw him was in the World Championship semi final at Leicester a few weeks later and by then he was going like a jet. I wonder whether maybe one or two things I'd told him had played some part in helping him along.

It's the old story, though. When a rider gets some success, and against good opposition, on the continent, there is no earthly reason why he shouldn't reproduce it at home. In fact, he is more likely to be flying in League matches simply because of the experience and confidence gained.

There was a rumour going around at Ipswich, apparently, which suggested that some of his slightly below-par early season returns were because he was spending too much time driving to and from the continent and worrying about his racing there. Nothing could be further from the truth. He took those continental meetings seriously enough, was always well organised, properly prepared, well turned out, good equipment and so on. But that's how he would be for English meetings as well, certainly any I caught up with. The bloke is a professional in every sense of the word.

It doesn't take much to tell about people. Loads of English boys have failed to fulfil their real potential simply because of their attitude. With so much racing in England there is always tomorrow but John rides like there is no such thing.

Not that he is a crazy man, just very aggressive and competitive. Sure, sometimes he has tended to

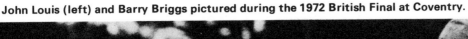

John Louis (left) and Barry Briggs pictured during the 1972 British Final at Coventry.

over-ride a little, but that isn't such a bad fault. When I think of some of my own early days and compare them with the way this boy 'over-rides', it's a laugh.

The important thing is that he doesn't go crashing all over the place, so obviously he isn't over-reaching too much. When you're coming up though, there is always something to prove and like any ambitious youngster worth his salt he wanted to prove that he could not just hold his own, but that he could beat any of us.

He did that in a later Italian meeting when he came back towards the latter part of the season. Ivan was there, too, and he'd just won the world's long track (1,000 metre) title for the second time, so he was on song and didn't entertain the idea of defeat. I was going a bit myself, too. The build-up for Wembley was in full swing and both physically and mentally I was getting myself built up for the big one.

Some people might think that this would involve putting aside all the minor meetings and concentrating on the big one. But the only way to concentrate on the big one is to work up to a high pitch at which both man and machinery are performing as sweetly as possible: so I wanted success in this Italian meeting as much as anything.

John blew his bike up after a winning start, but he didn't bat an eyelid when he had to meet Ivan and myself in his next race. The pressure was on, yet he just roared round the fence and blew us both off. I thought then that here was a real prospect . . . not just a bright boy but a rider who was going to make a big impact at the very highest level.

Officialdom . . . and fans

Remember, even at this stage, though he had qualified for the World Final, the speedway public at large still reckoned he was a bit of a fluke qualifier. He hadn't been capped by England in any of their Inter-Nations tournament matches and it seemed that everyone, everywhere – officialdom and fans – except at Ipswich, of course, reckoned that he was a five minute wonder.

The last couple of months of the season must have banished those ideas. In fact, the Tiger had a phenomenal finish to the year. He got 11 points a Wembley, and most people would have beer satisfied.

John wasn't. Some folk might have felt that thi was just conceit, and he didn't want that. But fo sure he was kicking himself simply because he hac started his first Final with a couple of grubby rides Even he had come to believe what most people thought . . . that really he was lucky just to be there let alone thinking about winning the title.

When you look back, however, it is easy to see that he might have picked up another couple of points in those first two races, and 13, remember, was the total with which Ivan won after a run-off with Bernie Persson. I don't think John's disappointment contained a shred of conceit, other than the sort of self-belief you have to have to be in with a chance of winning anything.

Difficult apprenticeship

This idea that you have to be around for years and must serve a long and difficult apprenticeship before having a chance of the big prizes is rubbish. If you learn fast enough, then you're ready. John started speedway later than most but this age business is immaterial. He had been racing for a few years and as it happened the fact that he didn't do speedway earlier has not been any hindrance to him.

Okay, so he was in his first Final but in many ways this could have been the best chance he will ever have ot winning the title. Nobody reckoned him, and because of the qualification system, there were a lot of strange Russians who logically shouldn't have been as tough opposition as if, say, half-a-dozen of the British League boys had been there. And with his temperament, a 75,000 Wembley crowd wasn't going to bother him – why should it, after all, when a big slice of them were rooting for him anyway?

My second World Final, in 1955, was one that got away. I scored a dozen points but if it hadn't been for a couple of mishaps I could have had the world's championship there and then.

Most riders thought I was an ungrateful so-and-so, grumbling about missing out when in fact everybody reckoned I had done well. But it took

Briggo riding in a sand-track meeting at Landshut in Bavaria, West Germany.

me another couple of years to get that world title, and at the time there was no telling whether this had been the great opportunity missed.

Probably John felt that way after Wembley '72 but his time can come again. That was one event which firmly established him in every eye as a rider of genuine world class, instead of just another fly-by-might interloper. His performances in a lot of the big open meetings in the closing weeks of the season, and in the World Cup Final in Olching . . . ironically is first international recognition . . . underlined the tremendous progress he had made.

Earlier in the season, victories he got in the First Division were a bonus; by the back-end it was a rarity if he dropped a point or two. This sort of transformation doesn't just happen by accident and the bloke means business, which is tough news for the rest of the boys.

Now he knows where he stands, and so does everybody else. But it doesn't bother the guy that now everybody wants to roll him over. It's the type of challenge he doesn't mind at all. Nor should he. It keeps you sharp, when everybody is out to beat you.

If he was a bit younger, maybe, John would not be able to cope quite so easily. But he's rubbed around a bit and I don't see him getting carried away with any juvenile flights of fantasy. If you have come through the mill, you can do without that sort of thing.

He has had two or three years of the Ipswich people heaping their praise on him and good luck to him for latching on to that. It's one of the bonuses you earn. If you can handle the Italians, you can handle anybody. After Montagnana, up on a truck being paraded through the town at half past eleven at night, with a rock-and-roll band in tow, it's hard not to feel like a celebrity.

But 'The Pope' knows that it doesn't just happen. You have to work hard at it. He accepts it. Some of the other English hopefuls could learn plenty from his attitude.

Meet the 'Briggo Boys'

In May, 1973, a new team burst upon the British scene . . . the 'Briggo Boys.' Five riders were chosen by Barry Briggs for what was to be a very special squad. He wanted one rider from New Zealand, one from Australia, one from America, one from England – plus Martin Ashby, with whom he had ridden for so long at Swindon. Each member of the team is sponsored by Briggo, receiving special leathers, helmets, mudguards, helmet-bags – in fact, all the products produced by Barry Briggs Racing. They have their own race-jackets and Barry takes a particular interest in their progress and development; rendering advice and the benefit of his own vast experience. Left to right: Scott Autrey, Graeme Stapleton, Dave Jessup, Martin Ashby, Barry Briggs.

TOP LEFT: Martin Ashby of Swindon and England — Briggo's first choice. Barry has always maintained that Martin could be England's number one. TOP RIGHT: Graeme Stapleton of Wimbledon and New Zealand — impressed Barry with his form in New Zealand during the last close season and a rider of great potential. BOTTOM LEFT: Dave Jessup of Leicester and England — recognised by Barry as one of England's outstanding prospects. BOTTOM RIGHT: From America, the choice was Scott Autrey, who quickly settled into the British League and has been a big hit with Exeter.

MIDDLE LEFT: Phil Crump of Kings Lynn and Australia who suffered a badly broken wrist before the season was in full swing and had a long stay out of the saddle. MIDDLE RIGHT: The 'skipper' who says: 'I chose these five in preference to riders who were already established in the top flight because I think with the right sort of help and encouragement they could get to the very top.'

An unusual shot of Briggo riding at the Santa Barbra track in California.

Frankie Shuter leads Ivan Mauger and Graeme Smith at a meeting in Christchurch, New Zealand.

**Men behind the masks —
Barry Briggs and Nigel
Boocock.**

**Chris Pusey, in some
magnificent leathers,
pictured riding in
New Zealand. The young
Belle Vue star was a big
hit with the Kiwi crowds.**

MAUGER by BRIGGS

'Some people make him out to be like a machine, but that isn't really the Ivan I know.'

There are times, when I read some of the things written about Ivan Mauger, when I really do begin to wonder whether he's human or some sort or robot. Some people make him out to be like a machine, but that's not really the Ivan I know.

I've travelled the world with the bloke, spent hours, days, weeks with him. And we've had a load of laughs. That's important. We Kiwis have a pretty zany sense of humour — right down from Trevor Redmond and Bruce Abernathy, perhaps the greatest character of them all, to Ivan.

But the colourful side of Ivan rarely gets an airing. Sure he's just about the most professional rider there is . . . works everything out, ice-cool when the pressure is on, leaves nothing to chance. Attention to detail is everything and it would be a surprise to find him making any silly mistakes on a World Final night, for example.

That's the Ivan Mauger most people know. Underneath all that, however, he's pretty much like the rest of us. Off the track, and especially away from it, Ivan and I have shared some great times . . . doing simple things but getting tremendous pleasure and amusement out of them.

Our trip to New Zealand earlier this year is a typical example. We lived like roaming gypsies for a while, moving from one place to another almost every day.

One day we arrived in Gisborne from Wanganui to be picked up by Gerry Hubert, the local PR man, and whisked off to his place for tea. Junie and Raye, Ivan's wife, were with us . . . and we had nowhere to stay. We were right on the fringe of some beautiful countryside, and in the midst of some great camping ground.

Gerry and his wife Lyn suggested we stay with them, but Ivan had another idea. "We'll camp," he said and that's exactly what we did. After racing at Gisborne, we came back, borrowed some tents and sleeping bags and set out to pitch camp.

It was terrific, but as Ivan thought of it he was put in charge of tea-making. I collected the wood, and we boiled some water in a billy-can and generally roughed it. There was a good deal of mickey-taking going on, and plenty of laughs, and it all helped take the pressure off and let us relax.

There's a touch of the 'Walter Mitty' about Ivan. I'm sure he'd like to be a cowboy really. He's always on about riding a horse across the hills at sunset, singing to a guitar. Not that he's got the greatest voice . . . as I well recall.

Some years ago, when we were with a British tourist team in Poland, Ivan performed a song and dance routine . . . on a banquet table! We were at a reception given by the Polish authorities. Our hosts provided some Polish schnapps . . . in about two seconds flat all the boys were pretty drunk.

They tell me it's potent stuff. I was sober, as the only non-drinker in the party. Suddenly, Ivan was up on the table, giving a pretty terrible impression of Johnny Devlin, a New Zealand pop singer. I walked alongside him, steering our budding pop star through the various dishes on the table.

I thought we were going to be in terrible trouble. It was then that I realised I was the only sober bloke in the place and Ivan's act seemed to go down pretty well!

Obviously Ivan and I are great rivals. But whenever I have motor trouble — and that's been no rarity in recent years — he's always the first one up to see if he can help me out. Mind you, before he hands over a bike he has to work hard covering up the special adjustments he's got on his machines.

We had a lot of laughs recalling what he's had to do to keep his secrets from me. On the track we race hell out of each other, but he'll ring me up asking what gear ratio to use at a certain track, or what tyre pressure, and I'll do the same.

While preparing to race in Hastings, New Zealand, we spent all day on the footpath tuning our bikes. My hands would be in his toolbox, his in mine . . . and all to beat each other. As soon as we're on the track, I want to lick him hollow. And that's just what he wants to do to me.

We're rivals, we respect each other, and we're mates too. That's good. I've always enjoyed my speedway. Not just the racing but the life that goes with it. Travelling around the country, across Europe and to the other side of the world can get tedious.

There's got to be a lighter side of it. A time for a joke and some laughs. Ivan and I have had a load of those.

Some rest for Ivan and Raye Mauger during a plane trip from one country to another.

MAUGER AND BRIGGS

Barry Briggs, with some last-minute mechanical adjustments, at his first speedway meeting in England in 1973 . . . the Daily Express Spring Classic at Wimbledon.

Barry Briggs and . . . who? Underneath the wig is World Champion Ivan Mauger.

Ivan Mauger and Barry Briggs share a joke during a meeting at Poole.

Ivan Mauger, on a long track circuit in West Germany.

International competition...

Changes must be made, says Barry -riders should be given greater incentive to wear their country's colours at home or abroad

I CAN never make up my mind whether British speedway cares about international competition or whether it's regarded as a bore and a chore. The promoters like their share of receipts from internationals, so much so that a few years ago almost every other match seemed to be tagged 'international'. In the end the public rumbled it, as they were bound to.

But the attitudes which still prevail are far from satisfactory. The lead should come from the top, yet I would say Great Britain's successes in the World Team Cup in the past few seasons have been due mostly to the determination of the boys who rode rather than any great encouragement from above.

Any professional worth his salt wants to make an impression, and especially so in top flight international competition. Bred as we are to go for individual success so much of the time, it isn't always easy to think about a team effort in quite the same way . . . and that isn't, repeat IS NOT, a New Zealander who just happens to have been selected for Great Britain doing the talking.

A lot of nonsense has been spoken and written about having Ivan, Ronnie and myself representing Great Britain. We have been pleased and proud to do so despite numerous knocks which suggested that an all-English team would have done so much better.

Well, for a long-time there were so few decent English riders around that people were more than pleased to have us along. And anyway, don't be fooled by the 'honorary' Briton bit. Take a look at my passport and you'll see that I have heard of The Queen as well.

Under the F.I.M., which controls world speedway, we are eligible to ride for Great Britain because New Zealand – and Australia – comes under the jurisdiction of the British Control Board. Maybe that's a quaint situation, and every so often there are rumbles from Down Under. Naturally the Australian and New Zealand authorities would like to be able to govern their own affairs; but it has to be admitted that even in this day and age of jet travel and all the rest, the meaningful speedway competition all happens on this side.

Whether that's right or wrong is a whole new argument: that's how it is. I strongly feel that the contribution blokes like Ivan and myself have made speaks for itself. We could both do without the old nonsense, but it goes on.

Mind you, we had to get annoyed to get ourselves going in the World Team Cup. For years it had been just one of those annual jaunts which nobody took desperately seriously. How could you when there was little money to be made and the arrangements frequently resembled Fred Karno's circus.

Great Britain's team which won the World Team Cup in Poland in 1971 . . . left to right Ronnie Moore, Barry Briggs, Ray Wilson, Jim Airey and Ivan Mauger.

But when the Poles and Swedes kept putting it over us, you couldn't help getting honked off about it. It really was a case of 'us' and 'them' and although we won the Cup at Wembley in 1968, coming very close to surprising the Poles in Rybnik the following year was an even better performance; losing it in spectacular style to a tremendously dedicated and fiercely committed Swedish team – at Wembley of all places – in 1970 was the rude jolt which shook everybody out of their complacency.

Winning the title in Wroclaw in 1971 was a great triumph and holding on to it at Olching last year was another one up for the boys.

But there has to be more to it than that. International competition and exchange must be a good thing and a few steps have been made in this direction. There's been the Internations tournament, the World League, and exchange visits but there must be more. British speedway – the promoters really and the public as well if we look at it closely – should be prepared to spare some of its stars for a spell so that if we want to send a side to **Sweden, or Poland, or Russia (say) for a fortnight or more, we can do so.**

Learning how the other half lives is a vital part of a speedway rider's education. This sort of education and experience is priceless.

Some of us had to educate ourselves by getting in on the continent and sampling other forms of racing. This practise will increase rather than decrease, no doubt, and the rewards in Europe are an added incentive . . . although a rider has to be prepared to start in a modest way and wait a while for the big rewards.

But just because that state of affairs applies when it's a private enterprise affair, it should not when the name of the game is international competition. It MUST be made sufficiently attractive for riders to want to go abroad on these trips.

The honour and the glory is all very fine but it's nowhere near enough. If an event has important status, then it's up to British speedway to make sure that its representatives are suitably rewarded. It is ludicrous to ask a man to ride in a supposedly major international event in which he may well end up earning far less than he would in an ordinary (and much easier) League meeting at home.

Because they don't stand to coin money out of sending teams abroad, the authorities at this end are reluctant to think in this way. But if you can understand or even sympathise in part with that state of affairs, how about big meetings in this country?

When a track stages a Test match or other all-star event, up go the prices of admission, programmes, etc. The boys get a bit more, true, but only in the basic rate. You have to work that much harder to earn a little extra, and for the unlucky guys who don't pick up too many points, they will go home less well paid than for a much easier domestic competition.

The time has come when events of those sort should carry a guarantee for each rider. After all, the public is coming to see the top names and therefore the pickings should be shared around a bit more.

We had all this out with the World Final last year. But that's another story. My point here is that if the boys are supposed to think big and do their bit on the international scene, it has to be elevated to top status by the people who control the purse strings. But that's not all. Organisation is still haphazard compared to the Poles and the Russians.

When we go to the big meetings on the continent these fellows have mechanics scurring everywhere, mountains of spares and all the rest. Anything we do looks puny by comparison and as often as not, there would be nothing for the boys unless one of us had geared up the arrangements.

Many times I've had my mechanic, Stan Palmer, load up a truck with bikes and other equipment and thus we have been able to compete on something approaching the same basis as the Eastern Europeans. But expecting one man or maybe two to look after the needs of four or five blokes in a big meeting is a joke.

Then again, you cannot really knock the other boys for not organising the full works themselves because the Control Board don't want to know about additional expense. And if each of the members of a World Team Cup team wanted to take his own mechanic and the amount of equipment you would normally have for a British League meeting, he would get no encouragment.

Even in this country it's heads I win, tails you lose. If an international is to mean anything surely it shouldn't be run in opposition to other meetings. Dates should be set aside on which matches are staged and that's it. From the point of view of attracting spectators, it's a must.

World Team Cup victors in 1968 . . . left to right Martin Ashby, Ivan Mauger, Barry Briggs, Nigel Boocock and Norman Hunter.

Most tracks run every week and don't want to miss. But if all domestic fixtures were ruled out for a week or a fortnight while the important matches are on, people would be persuaded to travel further to see internationals which meant something.

The World League this year is a step in the right direction, but too much is crammed into a short period of time and in the end people can have too much of a good thing. From the rider's point of view, clashes of interest between club matches and internationals should be avoided.

Certainly at the moment there isn't enough incentive for a rider, who stands to miss out on a home meeting where he would usually be expected to clean up, to give that away while he travels elsewhere for a tougher meeting – which doesn't guarantee to bring him the same sort of money.

Logically, though, the clash of interests should not be allowed to occur. With the season as long as it is, and getting longer each year it seems, surely the fixture list is not so congested that a compromise couldn't be reached.

Once upon a time internationals were something special. Now I'm not so sure. The only event which really qualifies as something special in the international calendar is the World Team Cup . . . which is where we came in. Although an addition in 1973 was the 'Daily Mirror International Tournament'.

Basically, I think the blokes themselves are as keen to keep the flag flying as any of the riders from Sweden, or Russia or Poland. It's just that the foreigners always seem to have everybody pulling for them, motivating them, encouraging them . . . and not just with words, either, but with tangible help.

As racing becomes more and more professional, the boys need something more than the assumption that British is best and therefore we don't have to work at it. Given the right lead we can't go wrong but if it isn't forthcoming the foreign threat is likely to provide a few rude jokes.

Great pals from New Zealand . . . Ivan Mauger (left), Briggo and Ronnie Moore.

Ole Olsen, World Champion in 1971, captured in pensive mood during the 1972 final at Wembley. Olsen won four races, but fell in his first heat.

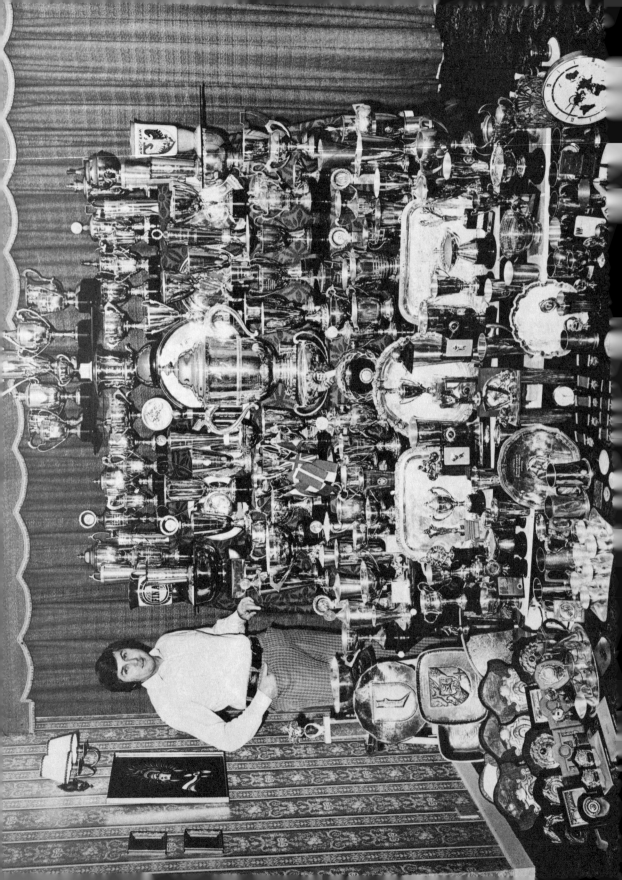

Trevor Redmond is always telling Barry Briggs that 'men were men in his day'. So we thought we would show a picture to prove it, showing Trevor in his hey-day, with the latest type of helmet and leathers. Note also the long-legs (now shrunk) and the usual slick Redmond car waiting to whisk him away; at least as far as the railway, where both he and car could cadge a lift! We're only joking Trevor!